Jorge Octavio Guzmán Sánchez

Web programming with Laravel

Jorge Octavio Guzmán Sánchez

Web programming with Laravel

getting to know the framework

Imprint

Any brand names and product names mentioned in this book are subject to trademark, brand or patent protection and are trademarks or registered trademarks of their respective holders. The use of brand names, product names, common names, trade names, product descriptions etc. even without a particular marking in this work is in no way to be construed to mean that such names may be regarded as unrestricted in respect of trademark and brand protection legislation and could thus be used by anyone.

Cover image: www.ingimage.com

This book is a translation from the original published under ISBN 978-620-2-12852-0.

Publisher:
Sciencia Scripts
is a trademark of
Dodo Books Indian Ocean Ltd. and OmniScriptum S.R.L publishing group

120 High Road, East Finchley, London, N2 9ED, United Kingdom
Str. Armeneasca 28/1, office 1, Chisinau MD-2012, Republic of Moldova, Europe
Printed at: see last page
ISBN: 978-620-7-19368-4

Contents

Credits

Jorge Octavio Guzman Sanchez is a professor in the department of Computer Systems Engineering at the Tecnologico Nacional de Mexico / IT in Tuxtla Gutierrez, where he teaches "Web Programming With Frameworks". Thanks to this, for several years he has been able to gather this knowledge in a text that can serve as teaching material for students studying the aforementioned subject.

1 Frameworks

I will start by commenting that this is not a book on object-oriented programming, but we will discuss the basic concepts of this paradigm. For several years I have seen that there is no text that contains most (or all) of the topics of the subject, students turn to the internet but find a lot of opinions y the idea of this writing arose to demonstrate application of concepts in LARAVEL.

Object-oriented programming

For the royal academy of the Spanish language a paradigm is a theory o set of theories whose central nucleus is accepted without question y that provides the basis y model to solve problems y advance in knowledge (among other meanings) but we will summarise it como "THE WAY OF THINKING", y a programming paradigm is como we think in the solution of a problem that we will then code to program.

In OOP what interests us are the objects involved in the process to be automated y that is why the first of the pillars (the first characteristic that we will see) is ABSTRACTION: which is a mental process by means of which we only take the aspects that in our opinion are relevant to the problem we are working on y with these we declare the classes in the programming language that is used.

The next pillar of OOP is ENCAPSULATION, which is a strategy with which we can define como be able to access the characteristics that we abstract from an entity.

y deteimma the way in which objects access them (here we will first identify the difference between class y object, the first is the declaration of the como is (como conforms), take como if it were a piano in a house y **object is the instance of a class,** in the example that we handle think that it is every time a house is built, in a subdivision are made several with the same pianos), y there are three levels, the two extremes are easy to assimilate the public y the private, in a class its attributes can be public o private to define the access that an object can have to these, for example if we define the class worker y we establish that a characteristic of this is salary we can also establish that it is private that is to say that any other object will not be able to have direct access to this property since it only belongs to the instance itself, to any other object it will not be able to be granted access.

The next pillar is the INHERITANCE this is a mechanism by which a class is allowed to be the basis for another (s) that will be (s) the (s) derived (s), here enters the not so correct terms of parent class y daughter class, The result of this is that the classes that inherit have the same characteristics of the class that was its base, but here enters the third level of encapsulation that was not named before the **protected** (private to others y public among the family).

Finally there is the POLYMORPHISM that is the ability to perform something in VARIOUS WAYS, suppose we have a base class called animal y one of its methods is to express itself, y craemos two classes one dog y another cat, both are classes derived from the animal class, both have a method that allows them to express themselves but we can implement that they express themselves in different ways the first will express itself barking y the second mauyando.

They are known como PILLARS of object-oriented programming since thanks to these strategies it is possible to code a complete program. As I said at the beginning "This is not a book of object oriented programming", it is only intended to make clear that these are necessary concepts to program with a framework because they are based on a language y the one we will work with is LARAVEL which uses PHP which is an object oriented language.

Since we are talking about programming issues we must remember the concept of design pattern since the framworks use it, we define this сото "a way of solving that is proven to work", this sentence is very generic, according to Gustavo Damian Campo who teaches at the Faculty of Engineering of the Catholic University of Salta, Argentina "A design pattern (design pattern) is a repeatable solution to a recurring problem in software design". (Campo, 2019), the most obvious is perhaps the MVC (Model-View-Controller Pattern), which I personally associate with the phrase "divide and conquer", the model that is the part that contains the logic of the application, commonly in this are the dates that are used in the solution of the problem (it is here where the database is accessed y in the majority of the frameworks of web development are linked to the handler of the database), the view is the part that determines сото these dates are shown to the user y the controller is the one who is in charge of deciding сото the system should react to the requests that the user makes to him.

This will be a book that will teach сото create an application using the LARAVEL framework, I emphasize once again that this is not a programming book so we will not delve into the subject, again is a reminder that the reader should investigate these issues.

We have mentioned the word framework on multiple occasions, Marcelo Ciceri in his book Introduction to Laravel: Robust and large-scale applications defines it as сото "a set of predefined and interconnected software structures and components that serve as the basis for the organisation and development of systems with general purposes" (Ciceri Vazquez, 2019). (Ciceri Vazquez, 2019) we understand that a framework is an incomplete but functional application (its function is typically a "hello world") y the programmer must modify (add other parts) to adapt it to the functional requirements of the client. There are different types of frameworks for all branches of knowledge, we take into account that this is a kind of gioser[1] in which the spaces are filled in a simple way (not to draw letters y foimar a text, but to achieve an objective) if it is a marketing framework is filled with the necessary actions to achieve the sale that is sought, if it is one of development the[1] objective is to create a program of certain characteristics so it will be added will be libraries y code that facilitates Hegar to the established objective.

As mentioned before there are multiple types of frameworks, the one we are interested in are the ones for web development, each one is based on a programming language, in the case of Java, we have

Spring, Struts y Serverlets, in the case of JavaScript we have Express y Nextjs y in the case of PHP we have Laravel, Symfony, Zend; All of the above lists are enunciative not limitative, in the same way there are frameworks that are known сото of front end y others are known сото of back end, these names make allusion to the part that these are executed, front end frameworks are found at the end that the end customer sees (these are those that modify the views y example of these is angular, vue y others) y others run on the server, there are times when the frameworks can be back o front, сото is the case of LARAVEL.

Another topic *to* discuss will be the tools we will use to create our development environment, first of all COMPOSER[2] , which is a dependency manager for php.

On several occasions you may have encountered a message that it is not possible to install software x because your computer is not installed software y (commonly happens if you want to install office y does not have the -.Net framework), this will no longer happen because your application will have a configuration file called composer.json (this is the configuration file is in JavaScript Object Notation format which is basically the way to describe multiple variables with their value), not to be confused with the file composer.lock, the first describes the **requirements** to be met for the installation of the application y in the second describes the packages that have been installed.

Another tool is git[3] which is a distributed version controller, this software allows you to keep track of the software files you develop, from time to time you perform "commits" which are сото "snapshots" to the code y these generate a unique identifier for each one (hash), at any time you can go back to a previous version (snapshot). The feature of distributed is because among varies users can make modifications to the same project (repository).

Another tool is ngrock[4] , it is an inverse proxy, that is to say that it is a software through which others can dispner of the resources that you establish, if you are developing a system with the help of a web server then in the port 80 of your machine will be able to see the result, but other people will not be able directly, they could configure so that they are in the same network y can see the system in your IP direction, but with ngrock a direction of the type http://fca2fa3fdl70 will be generated.ngrok.io and all the requests that anyone makes over the internet (if your friend uses that address) will enter the web application on your machine.

We will also talk about vagrant, it is a virtual environment manager, it requires a virtualizer (you can use oracle virtualbox or vmware or other) but you can create your own development environment, to continue we will demonstrate its use. As we explained before you can use a virtualizer but using vagrant we do not depend on any specific one, to be able to manage the virtual machines, these use an operative system y to install it ISO images are used, in the case of vagrant what is used are boxes (BOXes), The creators of the framework LARAVEL also created the BOX Homestead[5] , is an installation based on Ubuntu y has preloaded several tools (including those discussed above).

---

[3] You can download it at https://git-scm.com/downloads
[4] It can be found on their website https://ngrok.com/
[5] You can read https://laravel.eom/docs/9.x/homestead
5

```
●  ◉  ●        Homestead.yaml... — Modificado
---
ip: "192.168.10.10"
memory: 2048
cpus: 2
provider: virtualbox

authorize: ~/.ssh/id_rsa.pub

keys:
    - ~/.ssh/id_rsa

folders:
    - map: ~/code
      to: /home/vagrant/code

sites:
    - map: homestead.test
      to: /home/vagrant/code/public
    - map: prueba1.tst
      to: /home/vagrant/code/proyecto/public
      php: "7.4"
    - map: prueba2.local
      to: /home/vagrant/code/otro/public
      php: "8.0"

databases:
    - homestead

features:
    - mariadb: false
    - ohmyzsh: false
    - webdriver: false

#services:
#    - enabled:
#        - "postgresql@12-main"
#    - disabled:
#        - "postgresql@11-main"

# ports:
#    - send: 50000
#      to: 5000
#    - send: 7777
#      to: 777
#      protocol: udp
```

First we need to clone the laravel/homestead repository from github (in other words, we need to make a copy on our machine of the laravel user's homestead project that is on github). Next we will modify the configuration file Homestead.yalm (when we download our copy we can base it on the Homestead.yalm.example) to define coto we want the virtual machine to be, set the IP, how much ram memory we want to allocate and how many processors we want to share any folders from our host machine (physical machine) to our virtual machine, the above is declared in the **folders** section, where you will find a Hamada **map** entry which means that whatever we have in a certain location in our filesystem (the ~/**code)** means in the code subdirectory of the root directory of the current user (the user that is using Vagrant, remember that the directory we start in will be the one that contains our configuration file) y the **to** entry is the direction of where this folder will be (if you have used linux you may be familiar with the term mount a file system), there are other sections coto the **sites** section, which specifies the sites that our virtual machine will have, this then has preconfigured nginx with support for multiple hosts, each of them are configured according to the **sites** entries, an entry that you can apply is called php y this serves to establish the version of php that will have this site, you must remember that homstead depending on the version has installed multiple tools y also several versions of php, so I can declare that in test.test use php in version 7.4 y in test2.test use php in version 8 (the names of the sites are set with the entry **map** y the location of the files that will have this site are set with the entry **to)** there are several more sections but by configuring these you can create your development environment.

To start the virtual machine we use the command **vagrant up** y to shut it down we will use the **vagran halt,** every time we make a change in the configuration we will use the **vagrant reload -provision ,** it is important to use the modifier provision otherwise it would be сото "reset the machine but not to reload the confgiruacion that we modified.

Once we start our virtual machine (if you use your development environment with another tool, be it xamp, wamp, laragon, etc, you can use a terminal where you have command line access to the tools we will use, composer y php) we will enter it with **vagrant ssh** (remember that the vagrant tool should be run where you have the homestead configuration file).

2   First steps

First we will install the framework, to perform this action there are several ways, we will start by using the composer tool (which como we saw before is a dependency manager) that will read the file composer.json y in which are the requirements to install the application (remember that the file composer.lock contains the versions of the requirements that were already installed), if we review the contents of the file composer.json:

```
pruebas@otro:~/ejercicio$ cat composer.json
{
    "name": "laravel/laravel",
    "type": "project",
    "description": "The Laravel Framework.",
    "keywords": ["framework", "laravel"].
    "license": "MIT",
    "require": {
        "php": "^8.0.2",
        "guzzlehttp/guzzle": "^7.2",
        "laravel/framework": "^9.19",
        "laravel/sanctum": "^3.0",
        "laravel/tinker": "^2.7"
    },
    "require-dev": {
        "fakerphp/faker": "^1.9.1",
        "laravel/pint": "^1.0",
        "laravel/sail": "^1.0.1",
        "mockery/mockery": "^1.4.4",
        "nunomaduro/collision": "^6.1",
        "phpunit/phpunit": "^9.5.10",
        "spatie/laravel-ignition": "^1.0"
    },
    "autoload": {
        "psr-4": {
            "App\\": "app/",
            "Database\\Factories\\": "database/factories/",
            "Database\\Seeders\\": "database/seeders/"
        }
    },
    "autoload-dev": {
        "psr-4": {
            "Tests\\": "tests/"
        }
    },
    "scripts": {
        "post-autoload-dump": [
            "Illuminate\\Foundation\\ComposerScripts::postAutoloadDump",
            "@php artisan package:discover --ansi"
        ],
        "post-update-cmd": [
            "@php artisan vendor:publish --tag=laravel-assets --ansi --force"
        ],
        "post-root-package-install": {
            "@php -r \"file_exists('.env') || copy('.env.example', '.env');\""
        ],
        "post-create-project-cmd": [
            "@php artisan key:generate --ansi"
        ]
    },
    "extra": {
        "laravel": {
            "dont-discover": []
        }
    },
    "config": {
        "optimize-autoloader": true,
        "preferred-install": "dist",
        "sort-packages": true,
        "allow-plugins": {
            "pestphp/pest-plugin": true
        }
    },
    "minimum-stability": "dev",
    "prefer-stable": true
}
pruebas@otro:~/ejercicio$ 
```

We found that re requisite to have the version 8.0.2 o superior of php as well como the 9.19 o superior of freamework, y some other requistos but, so when we use the tool will check y download these, firstly to install we will use the tool composer, with her we can create a project, even tell him in which version we want:

```
pruebas@otro:~$ composer create-project laravel/laravel="5.1.*" ejercicio
Creating a "laravel/laravel=5.1.*" project at "./ejercicio"
Installing laravel/laravel (v5.1.33)
  - Installing laravel/laravel (v5.1.33): Extracting archive
Created project in /home/pruebas/ejercicio
> php -r "copy('.env.example', '.env');"
Loading composer repositories with package information
Updating dependencies
Lock file operations: 58 installs, 0 updates, 0 removals
  - Locking classpreloader/classpreloader (3.2.1)
  - Locking danielstjules/stringy (1.10.0)
  - Locking dnoegel/php-xdg-base-dir (0.1)
  - Locking doctrine/inflector (1.4.4)
  - Locking doctrine/instantiator (1.4.1)
  - Locking fzaninotto/faker (v1.5.0)
  - Locking hamcrest/hamcrest-php (v1.2.2)
  - Locking jakub-onderka/php-console-color (v0.2)
  - Locking jakub-onderka/php-console-highlighter (v0.3.2)
```

For the previous example we are indicating that we want to create a project based on the laravel/laravel repository (coto before we commented is user/repository) we want version 5.1, but this is not the best since the version we want is already obsolete so we will install the current version.

```
pruebas@otro:~$ composer create-project laravel/laravel ejercicio
Creating a "laravel/laravel" project at "./ejercicio"
Installing laravel/laravel (v9.3.9)
  - Installing laravel/laravel (v9.3.9): Extracting archive
Created project in /home/pruebas/ejercicio
> @php -r "file_exists('.env') || copy('.env.example', '.env');"
Loading composer repositories with package information
Updating dependencies
Lock file operations: 107 installs, 0 updates, 0 removals
  - Locking brick/math (0.10.2)
  - Locking dflydev/dot-access-data (v3.0.1)
  - Locking doctrine/inflector (2.0.6)
  - Locking doctrine/instantiator (1.4.1)
  - Locking doctrine/lexer (1.2.3)
  - Locking dragonmantank/cron-expression (v3.3.2)
  - Locking egulias/email-validator (3.2.1)
  - Locking fakerphp/faker (v1.20.0)
  - Locking filp/whoops (2.14.5)
```

But there is an installer that was developed by the people who created the framework, we install it with the command:

```
pruebas@otro:~$ composer create-project laravel/installer
Creating a "laravel/installer" project at "./installer"
Installing laravel/installer (v4.2.17)
  - Installing laravel/installer (v4.2.17): Extracting archive
Created project in /home/pruebas/installer
Loading composer repositories with package information
Updating dependencies
Lock file operations: 37 installs, 0 updates, 0 removals
  - Locking doctrine/instantiator (1.4.1)
  - Locking myclabs/deep-copy (1.11.0)
  - Locking nikic/php-parser (v4.15.1)
  - Locking phar-io/manifest (2.0.3)
  - Locking phar-io/version (3.2.1)
  - Locking phpunit/php-code-coverage (9.2.17)
  - Locking phpunit/php-file-iterator (3.0.6)
  - Locking phpunit/php-invoker (3.1.1)
  - Locking phpunit/php-text-template (2.0.4)
  - Locking phpunit/php-timer (5.0.3)
```

As we did not specify a name for the folder at the end it will create a Hamada installer, inside it is the installer.

```
pruebas@otro:~$ ls
installer
pruebas@otro:~$ ls installer/
bin  ccmposer.json  composer.lock  LICENSE.md  README.md  src  vendor
pruebas@otro:~$ ls installer/bin/
laravel
pruebas@otro:~$
```

Using this one we can also install it with this one

```
pruebas@otro:~$ ./installer/bin/laravel new ejercicio



  | |                              | |
  | |    __ _  _ __  __ _ __   __ ___| |
  | |   / _` || '__|/ _` |\ \ / // _ \ |
  | |__| (_| || |  | (_| | \ V /|  __/ |
  |_____\__,_||_|   \__,_|  \_/  \___|_|


Creating a "laravel/laravel" project at "./ejercicio"
Info from https://repo.packagist.org: #StandWithUkraine
Installing laravel/laravel (v9.3.9)
  - Installing laravel/laravel (v9.3.9): Extracting archive
Created project in /home/pruebas/ejercicio
> @php -r "file_exists('.env') || copy('.env.example', '.env');"
Loading composer repositories with package information
Updating dependencies
Lock file operations: 107 installs, 0 updates, 0 removals
  - Locking brick/math (0.10.2)
  - Locking dflydev/dot-access-data (v3.0.1)
  - Locking doctrine/inflector (2.0.6)
  - Locking doctrine/instantiator (1.4.1)
  - Locking doctrine/lexer (1.2.3)
```

But we will do it step by step,, for this we will clone it using git

```
pruebas@otro:~$ git clone https://github.com/laravel/laravel.git ejercicio
Cloning into 'ejercicio'...
remote: Enumerating objects: 33557, done.
remote: Counting objects: 100% (1/1), done.
remote: Total 33557 (delta 0), reused 0 (delta 0), pack-reused 33556
Receiving objects: 100% (33557/33557), 10.25 MiB | 3.47 MiB/s, done.
Resolving deltas: 100% (19855/19855), done.
```

This creates a directory called exercise which contains the framework, but we still need some details to be able to use it, first we must create a general configuration file for the framework, this is the .env file y for this we can use the .env.example file (in unix based operating systems the files whose names begin with a dot are hidden).

With the following command **cp** we will make a copy of the **.env.example** file (remember that it must be in the exercise folder, you can do it from a file explorer as well).

It is time to install the dependencies, for this we will use the composer tool, we can see the composer.json file that is among the files that were downloaded, if you check it you will find that it states as required the laravel/framework package (we already commented as read this is user/repository).

```
pruebas@otro:~/ejercicio$ cat composer.json
{
    "name": "laravel/laravel",
    "type": "project",
    "description": "The Laravel Framework.",
    "keywords": ["framework", "laravel"],
    "license": "MIT",
    "require": {
        "php": "^8.0.2",
        "guzzlehttp/guzzle": "^7.2",
        "laravel/framework": "^9.19",
        "laravel/sanctum": "^3.0",
        "laravel/tinker": "^2.7"
    },
```

the command we will use to check if we have the requirements installed is update.

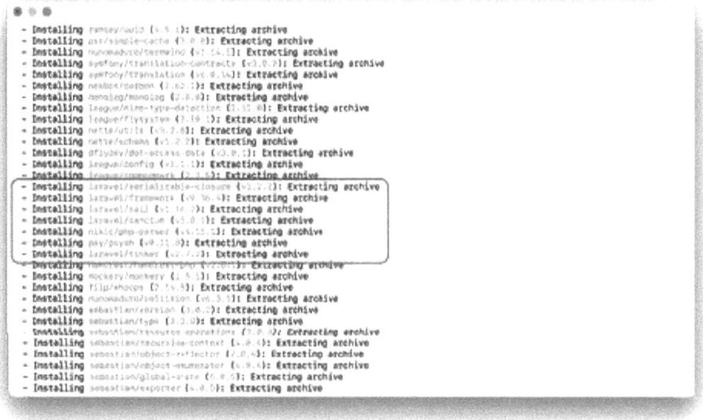

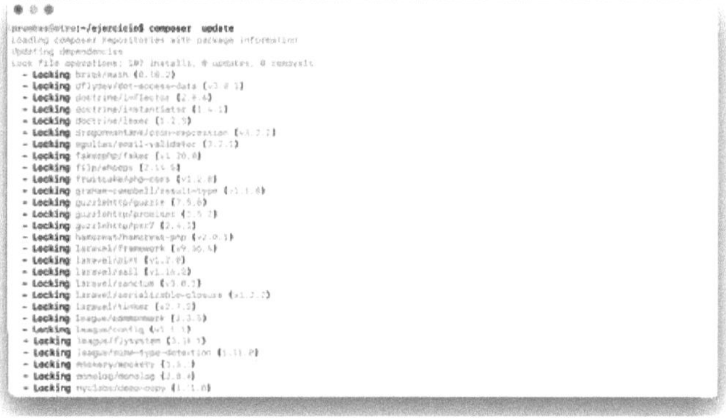
pruebas@otro:~/ejercicio$ composer update

- Locking myclabs/deep-copy (1.11.0)

Laravel handles a certain level of security so it uses a token based on a Have encryption (if the reader is not familiar with these issues it is recommended to read about public key encryption systems) so now we will use the framework's artisan script to generate this Have.

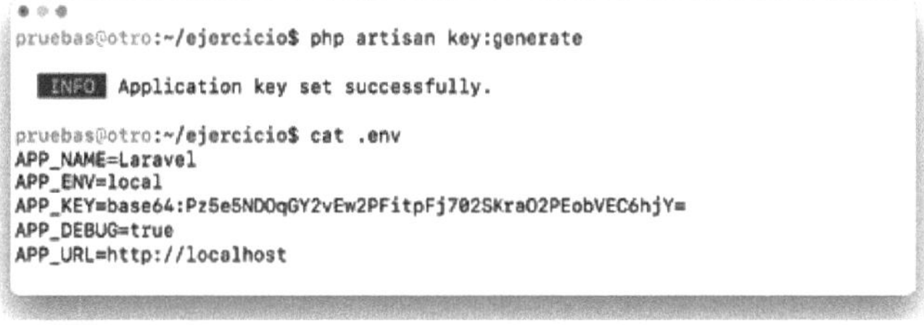
pruebas@otro:~/ejercicio$ php artisan key:generate
INFO Application key set successfully.
pruebas@otro:~/ejercicio$ cat .env
APP_NAME=Laravel
APP_ENV=local
APP_KEY=base64:Pz5e5NDOqGY2vEw2PFitpFj702SKraO2PEobVEC6hjY=
APP_DEBUG=true
APP_URL=http://localhost

I was able to confirm that the MAIL_ENCRYPTION variable in the .env file has changed from a clean string to a base 64 string.

We will explain the above command, first we call the php interpreter since artisan is a script in this language.

Artisan is the main script with which we can create elements, perform actions, etc... in other words manage LARAVEL.

The parameter key is the command to which after the colon we indicate the subcommand, in this case the Have we are generating (key has no variety of subcommands como others e.g. make).

Now that we have configured the framework we can see the framework in action, for this we will use the serve command (what this does is to make the framework raise a development web server), it installs it on port 8000 (unlike a web server which is usually on port 80), it installs it on port 8000 (unlike a web server which is usually on port 80), it installs it on port 8000 (unlike a web server which is usually on port 80).

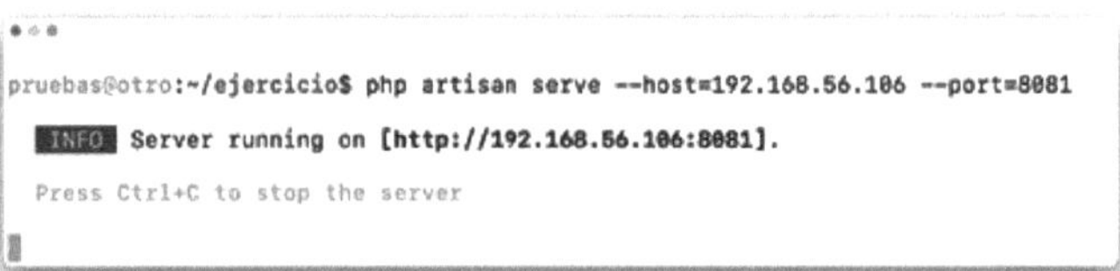

We can change the ip (it could be the one your machine has on the network it is on) y we can change the port as well.

y will now be able to view our system from a web browser.

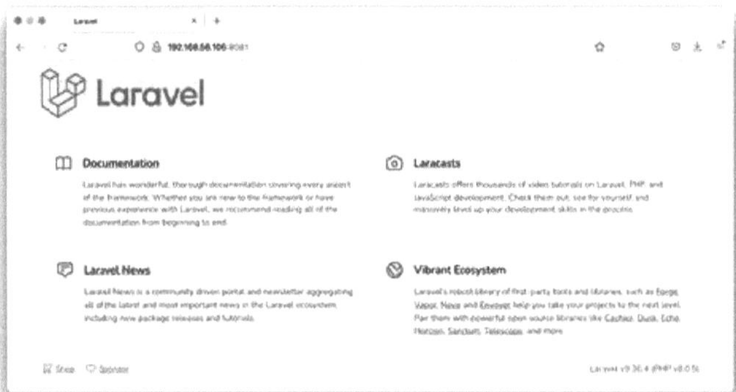

Note, when we created the exercise (either with the installer or with the composer tool) we ran all the steps, installed dependencies, generated the .env file and added the encryption key. As an exercise it is proposed to the reader to configure your web server so that by means of virtual hosts it allows the use of several projects simultaneously. If you are using WAMP, LAMP, LARAGON or some other server, at the end of the day it has a virtual host feature that allows you to define a server for different URLs that are associated to a different source code folder.

It's time to get to know the framework's y archives folders, for this we will explore the framework

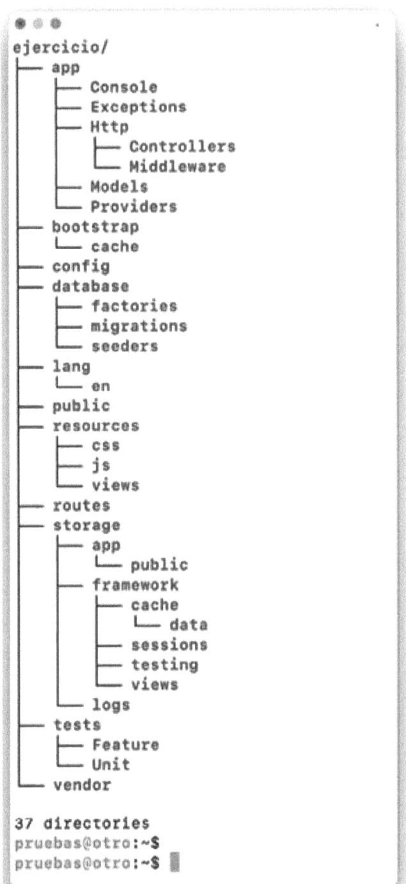

We will start by explaining the framework directories,   then we will explain the important files

First of all we have the app directory, we can say that the application (or most of it) will be inside this directory, it is here where we have a directory for commands, these are the ones we can execute with the artisan script, laravel already has several, we can create our own, next is the Exceptions directory where we will put the code that we want to be executed when an exception is encountered (as in several languages we use the try-catch, we can define the logic with which we will deal with that error y we can also define how the system will look like.

We have the Http folder, which contains the Controllers and Middlware folders, the first will contain the controllers (which are the classes that define the behaviour that the system will have when faced with certain requests), and the second is the folder in which the filters to the patitions will be stored, in

Here we can determine what the system will do when faced with a certain request, this is where we can validate if certain conditions are met, for example if the request is of a certain direction.

We continue inside the app with the **Models** folder (ignoring the User.php model that by default already exists in the installation) here are saved the models generated for our systems, commonly the models are those that are responsible for saving the data used in our application in the case of LARAVEL these work with the database through eloquent which is the (ORM[VI]) that uses the framework. In previous versions there was no special folder to store them.

Finally we find a folder to store the **Providers,** the installation already has some classes, these providers are responsible for configuring and loading some aspects of the application, we commonly say that in the app folder is the system (or at least most of it) because as we create events, emails and other aspects the code that is generated will be in sub folders of this (most of the classes that are created). The next folder to anlizar is bootstrap (this is a folder of the framework for the initialization of the application, not to be confused with the bootstrap of css).

The next folder is the configuration folder, this one is called **config** y inside it we will find php files (classes that take up arrangements with the configuration that certain parts of the system must have).

We have arrived at the **database** folder, in this folder we find the database configurations, we find three sub folders, the first one we will analyze is **migrations** because it is here where we define each of the components of the database, the next one is **seeders** which is here where we feed the data of our database (this is a mechanism to create for example a "default" user o if for example we were developing a system of car parts it would be necessary to have a catalog with the brands of cars, y is where we could feed this table) y lastly we will analyse the **factories** folder, it is through these that we can populate our database with records for testing, generally this is also done with seeders as usually the factories generate random data.

We continue with the **lang** folder that has a sub folder **in,** this is to be able to handle several languages for the application, by default the application works in the english language but this is possible to change it in the configuration (archive app.php that is in the config directory), in internet you will find open source projects to be able to change the language of the application, that is to add a sub folder.

It is time to check the **public** folder which is the starting point of our application, if you put any files inside it they will be available to anyone across the network, the web server defines this como the home folder.

The folder resources como its name indicates it contains the resources used by the application, it contains three sub folders, the first one that we will analyze is views y in it como its name indicates it we will include the pages that will be the "view" of our application, these will be rendered como html in the web browser of who uses our system; the other two folders (js *y* css) are used by a "preprocessor" currently LARAVEL uses VITE to generate the files app.js y app.css files with the resources used by our application y places them in the public folder (in previous versions it used webpack, but we can not use it and include our "assets" directly).

The next folder is **routes,** this directory contains the files api.php, channels.php, console.php y web.php, y in them we will define how the system will react to the requests that a user makes. It is possible to define the file in which to search for routes depending on the type of application that is handled, for example if it is a web application when the user enters the URL http://servidor/amigos/listar search the route in the file web.php which is located within

---

^{VI} Object Relational Mapping, is a way of programming in which all the elements of the database are mapped to object oriented programming, later we will deal with this topic in detail.

this folder y in this poremos poriri define the action to be carried out)

In the list the next directory is **storage,** y its function is to store, but it depends on the sub folder it uses, the ones we have are app, framework, y logs, the content of the **framework** folder (and its sub directories) are files that LARAVEL uses, for example the views compiled in php, the session files that are handled, etc., the **logs** folder contains the log files that the system generates, per defeto there is a file called laravel.log in which the errors that are generated are registered, y we have the **app** folder in which we save files that are stored in our application, for example files with photos that we can upload.

The **tests** folder contains two sub folders **Feature** y **Unit,** this is where we can save the files that define our purebas that will be performed to the system, these are functionality tests o unit tests.

And now we have the **vendor** folder in which we don't actually save files, this is the folder in which the libraries that are necessary to run the application are saved, remember the composer tool downloads all the requirements y if you modify any file that is inside the vendor the next time composer updates it will download new files y overwrite the changes.

When we talk about the special files that are in the root of the project we will find the files: composer.json, composer.lock, package.json, phpunit.xml, README.md y vite.config.js, of the first two we have already explained, the third one is to npm[VII] as the first one to the composer tool, we also have the case of an xml file in which the testing system of the framework is configured, the penultimate as its name suggests has information about the project y the last one is the configuration that allows to complete the assets (resources in java script y in css that will be included in the project, after the compilation with vite (in previous versions of laravel we used webpack) this is not necessary since the files app.css y app.js files that are generated with the compilation y will be located in public, it is possible to replace it with libraries or cdn's to these.

It is time to talk more in depth about routes, examples will be given with web routes (but similarly a web application can create routes for an API or others that LARAVEL handles).

In the /routes/web.php file, the ROUTE facade is included by default in the /routes/web.php file;

```
use Illuminate\Support\Facades\Route;
```

with this instruction we are saying that in the code of this file we can use the ROUTE class that is defined in this address (if we are observant we are referring to a file located in the vendor folder specifically /laravel/framework/src/Illuminate/Support/Facades/Route.php y if we observe is part of the framework, this class allows us to define new routes, ie when a user writes in the web client an "address" (ie a URL[VIII]) the actions to be performed, for this it is important to know what the **http verbs** are (in this writing only mention GET, PUT, POST y DELETE although there are many others).

For example we declare this route

```
Route::get('saludar',function(){
   echo "HOLA";
});
```

[VII] Acronym of node pakage manager, a node package manager (which is based on java script).
[VIII] Uniform Resource Locator commonly known as coto web address, is the one we see in the address bar of the browser.
{

That is indicating with an anonymous function that when the system receives a GET request that matches the URI "greet", it should print the word hello.

In this way we could receive by parameter the name of the person we are going to greet.

```
Route::get('saludar/{nombre}',function($parametro){
    $nombre = $parametro;
    echo "HOLA ";
    echo strtoupper($nombre);

});
```

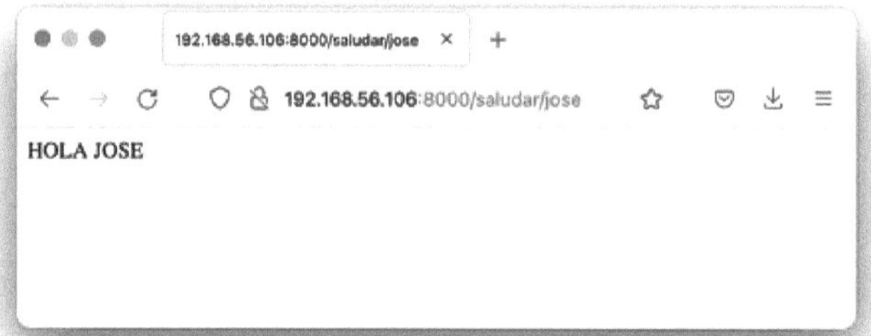

We can also pass another parameter which is the language in which we want to greet (English, French, Spanish).

```
Route::get('saludar/{nombre}/{idioma}',function($parametro01, $parametro02){
    $nombre = $parametro01;
    $idioma = $parametro02;
    switch ($idioma) {
```

```php
    case 'ingles':
        echo "HI ";
        echo strtoupper($nombre);
        break;
    case 'frances':
        echo "SALUT ";
        echo strtoupper($nombre);
        break;
    case 'aleman':
        echo "HALLO ";
        echo strtoupper($nombre);
        break;
    default:
        echo "USTED NO HA ESPECIFICADO ALGUN IDIOMA ";
        break;
    }
});
```


But if we do not introduce the language, the system gives an error, this is because we must remember that in the definition of the route we stated that the second parameter was not optional.

We solve this by defining the second optional parameter сото, y to the variable <u>we will give a default value.</u>

```
Route::get('saluda/{nombre}/{idioma?}',function($parametro01, $parametro02='español'){
    $nombre = $parametro01;
    $idioma = $parametro02;
    switch ($idioma) {
        case 'ingles':
            echo "HI ";
            echo strtoupper($nombre);
            break;
        case 'frances':
            echo "SALUT ";
            echo strtoupper($nombre);
            break;
        case 'aleman':
            echo "HALLO ";
            echo strtoupper($nombre);
            break;
        case 'español':
            echo "HOLA ";
            echo strtoupper($nombre);
            break;
    }
});
```


So far we have solved everything from our archive web.php but our system will continue to grow, we will add the functionality to ask for user y password, based on these credentials welcome the user o indicate that something was wrong, for this we will make a controller, these are used to group functionalities сото in the example we will see y can arise from two origins, a use case o the management of a model.

Partially the use case for logging in is:

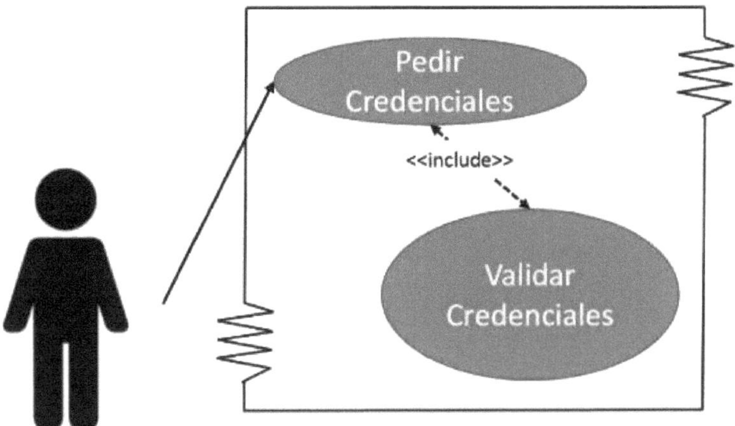

So we will create the controller called EntrarController (the convention says that the name will be in PascalCase y ending with the word Controller) so we will use the command :

```
php artisan make:controller EntrarController
```

that generates the file EntrarController.php that contains the class EntrarController y is in the folder **Controllers** that is a sub folder of **Http** that is in **app,** in this class we will create the methods requestCredentials, validateCredentials y exit (all these will be named using camel case[IX]) y in these methods we will include the code that generates the desired functionality. In this way our web.php file will have nothing more than the reference to the method we want to execute when a route is fulfilled.

Instead of using several lines of code (como is done on lines 21 to 40 which was the greeting path we used in previous examples) we use a few lines for the paths on lines 51 and 52 but we will add features to these later (we created the product and dashboard paths only as a test).

[IX] A notation style in which the first letter of each word is capitalised (everything else in lower case) to avoid using spaces, but unlike pascalcase the first letter of the result will be lower case.

```
20    Route::get('saludar/{nombre}/{idioma?}',function($parametro01, $parametro02='español'){
21        $nombre = $parametro01;
22        $idioma = $parametro02;
23        switch ($idioma) {
24            case 'ingles':
25                echo "HI ";
26                echo strtoupper($nombre);
27                break;
28            case 'frances':
29                echo "SALUT ";
30                echo strtoupper($nombre);
31                break;
32            case 'aleman':
33                echo "HALLO ";
34                echo strtoupper($nombre);
35                break;
36            case 'español':
37                echo "HOLA ";
38                echo strtoupper($nombre);
39                break;
40        }
41    });
42
43    Route::get('dashboard', function () {
44        echo "dashoard del administrador";
45    });
46
47    Route::get('productos', function () {
48        echo "mostar productos al cliente";
49    });
50
51    Route::get('entrar', [\App\Http\Controllers\EntrarController::class,'pedirCredenciales']);
52    Route::post('entrar', [\App\Http\Controllers\EntrarController::class,'validarCredenciales']);
53
```

We can optimise lines 51 y 52 by including the controller at the beginning of the web.php file with a [X][XI][XII][XIII][XIV]

```
1    <?php
2
3    use Illuminate\Support\Facades\Route;
4    use App\Http\Controllers\EntrarController;
5
```

```
48    Route::get('productos', function () {
49        echo "mostar productos al cliente";
50    });
51    Route::get('entrar', [EntrarController::class,'pedirCredenciales']);
52    Route::post('entrar', [EntrarController::class,'validarCredenciales']);
53
```

Something that we must comment is that in LARAVEL from version 8 the namespace of the routes that the system used by default was eliminated, in previous versions we could define the rat of the line 51 сото.

```
Route::get('entrar','EntrarController@pedirCredenciales');
```

And in version 8 it would be

```
Route::get('entrar','App\Http\Controllers\EntrarController@pedirCredenciales');
```

What is currently growing in code is the controller, which we will explain:

X <?php

XI

XII   use IlluminateXSupportXFacadesXRoute;

XIII   pse AppXHttpXControllersXEntrarController;

XIV

Route::get('products', function () {
echo "show products to customer";
});|
Route::get('enter',[EnterController::class,'requestCredentials']);
Route:: post('ent rar', [EntrarController:: class, 'validate reden cials']);

```php
1   <?php
2
3   namespace App\Http\Controllers;
4
5   use Illuminate\Http\Request;
6
7   class EntrarController extends Controller
8   {
9       function pedirCredenciales(){
10          echo "<html><head><title>ENTRADA</title></head><body>";
11          echo "<form method='post'>usuario:<input type='text' name='usr'><br>";
12          echo "clave:<input type='password' name='pwd'><br>";
13          echo "<input type='submit' value='enviar'></form></body></html>";
14      }
15      function validarCredenciales(Request $request){
16          $usuario = $request->input('usr');
17          $password = $request->input('pwd');
18          // Revisar si el usuario introdujo la clave correcta.
19          if ($usuario == 'admin' && $password == 'nimda')
20              return redirect('dashboard');
21          if ($usuario == 'cliente' && $password == 'etneilc')
22              return redirect('productos');
23          return redirect()->back();
24      }
25  }
26
```

What we have added is from line 9 to line 24, the rest is generated by the make:controller command.

In line 9 we create the method requestCredentials that with several Hamadas to the function echo of php we print a web page with a form that captures the user name (in a text box Hamada usr y the key in a text box of type password that is called pwd), to the formaulario we have assigned the method POST (remember what you know of the verbs http) coto we have not assigned attribute acction the destination of the data here acquired will be the same rat.

At this point, in order for the POST data sending to work, we must comment out the use of the middleware VerifyCsrfToken in the web key of the middlewareGroups array of the app/Http/Kemel.php file.

```php
28       *
29       * @var array<string, array<int, class-string|string>>
30       */
31      protected $middlewareGroups = [
32          'web' => [
33              \App\Http\Middleware\EncryptCookies::class,
34              \Illuminate\Cookie\Middleware\AddQueuedCookiesToResponse::class,
35              \Illuminate\Session\Middleware\StartSession::class,
36              \Illuminate\View\Middleware\ShareErrorsFromSession::class,
37              //\App\Http\Middleware\VerifyCsrfToken::class,
38              \Illuminate\Routing\Middleware\SubstituteBindings::class,
39          ],
40
41          'api' => [
42              // \Laravel\Sanctum\Http\Middleware\EnsureFrontendRequestsAreStateful::class,
43              'throttle:api',
44              \Illuminate\Routing\Middleware\SubstituteBindings::class,
45          ],
46      ];
47
```

It is time to explain the validateCredentials method that begins on line 15 of our file

EntrarController, we can see that in the signature of the method we find that receives como parameter the request (the request sent by the client to the server)[xv] current, with this we can identify the origin of the request, so como the variables that come in it.

Then in line 16 we will get what the user wrote in the text box called usr (similar to what is done in the code that follows, but now does it with the input pwd), the logic we use for validation is extremely simple, if the user that was introduced is called **admin** y with password **nimda we** allow him to see the dashboard of the application, similarly if the user is called **client** y his password is the word **etneilc** he will be able to see the page of products, for that reason we use the function redirect y to this we pass como parameter the route to which we want to direct the system. But if the credentials entered are not correct, then the system will be redirected to the previous step (remember that before we were in the input form).

But we have not yet teiminado, it turns out that although we now have a web.php file that is understandable everything we have piled up in the controller y is time to use the views. For this there is no command make:view, are files that we create y can be scripts in php o in blade (the latter is the template system that includes LARAVEL), has a special directory in which to save y this is called **views** which is located in the **resources** folder of our project.

We can deerr that Blade is como php to HTML, while the latter limits the use of variables y control structures (among other features) y the former also adds other peculiarities, for example, sanitization of data (use php's htmlspecialchars function to prevent xss attack, if you want to print a variable tai como comes you can use `{!! $variable !!}`), so como other directives (in the cycles you have access to the variable `$loop` gives you information about the iterations) y other features more.

At this point we can define the view that is called ask (actually is to create a php file called ask.php that later we will convert into ask.blade.php) that is inside the folder views, in this file we will write what would be an html page that asks for the two fields, if the old content of the method askCredentials as this now only return the instruction to load this view.

```php
function pedirCredenciales(){
    return view('pedir');
}
```

```html
1   <!DOCTYPE html>
2   <html lang="es">
3   <head>
4       <meta charset="UTF-8">
5       <meta http-equiv="X-UA-Compatible" content="IE=edge">
6       <meta name="viewport" content="width=device-width, initial-scale=1.0">
7       <title>Document</title>
8   </head>
9   <body>
10      <form method="post">
11          usuario: <input type="text" name="usr"><br>
12          clave: <input type="password" name="pwd"><br>
13          <input type='submit' value='enviar'>
14      </form>
15  </body>
16  </html>
```

Ilustración 1 Order.php file code

The behaviour of the system remains the same, but we have managed to separate the elements

---

of the programme, so that we can now assign the views to a designer (or someone who specialises in UX/UI) and let someone else work on the programming (the validation code).

But the features that the framework offers us are many y we are just getting to know them, coгo before I mentioned there is blade, y we can define that this is what php to html, y so instead of the file request has the extension php now will be a file ".blade.php" (there is precedence if there are several files that are called the same but have different extensions one is html, another php y another is blade.php then the view function will load the last type of file before the second y before the third), if we want to pass some variable to the view we define this can be done in several ways, one of them is to use the php compact function y then assign it as a parameter to the view.

Now our method would look like this:

```
function pedirCredenciales(){
    $sistema = "EJEMPLO";
    return view('pedir', compact('sistema'));
}
```

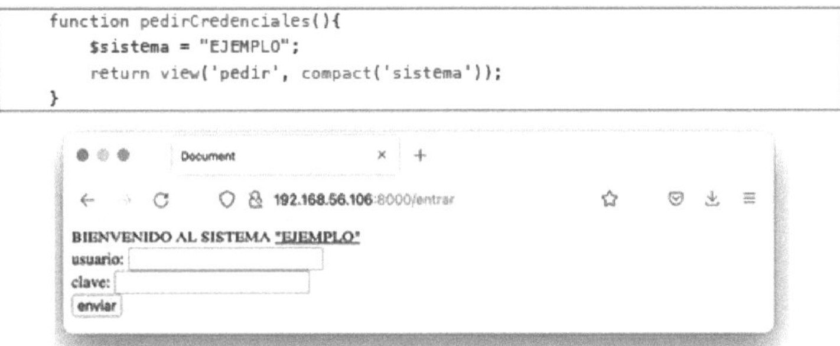

And the view was like this:

```
1   <!DOCTYPE html>
2   <html lang="es">
3   <head>
4       <meta charset="UTF-8">
5       <meta http-equiv="X-UA-Compatible" content="IE=edge">
6       <meta name="viewport" content="width=device-width, initial-scale=1.0">
7       <title>Document</title>
8   </head>
9   <body>
10      BIENVENIDO AL SISTEMA <u>"{{$sistema}}"</u>
11      <form method="post">
12          usuario: <input type="text" name="usr"><br>
13          clave: <input type="password" name="pwd"><br>
14          <input type='submit' value='enviar'>
15      </form>
16  </body>
17  </html>
```

Another aspect that we will see will be the models, LARAVEL uses eloquent so if we run the command **php artisan make:model Conocido** the file Conocido.php is generated in the sub directory Models of the folder app (the convention marks that the names of the models will be in pascal case y in singular, really they make mention to the entity).

But coгo we will not use databases yet we do not need neither to inherit from Model nor to use the trait[XVI] HasFactory so we can remove the references to these classes y instead we will put: the session array, for this we first take all the dates that are saved, we update the element of the array that is currently working with the value in memory y already updated the array is

---

[XVI] A php strategy to allow multiple inheritance similar to the implementation of an interface, gives to an attribute o method the possibility to be executed in the class context not in the instance context, that is to say that it allows to make changes but at a generic level, not at a specific one.

saved again in the session.

```php
1    <?php
2    namespace App\Models;
3
4    class Conocido{
5        public $id;
6        public $nombre;
7        static public function all(){
8            return session('datos',[ ]);
9        }
10       public function save(){
11           $datos = session('datos',[]);
12           $datos[$this->id]=$this->nombre;
13           session(['datos' => $datos]);
14           return true;
15       }
16       static public function  find($id){
17           $datos = session('datos',[]);
18           if(isset($datos[$id])){
19               $nuevo = new Conocido();
20               $nuevo->id = $id;
21               $nuevo->nombre = $datos[$id];
22               return $nuevo;
23           }else{
24               return null;
25           }
26       }
27       static public function delete($id){
28           $datos = session('datos',[]);
29           unset($datos[$id]);
30           session(['datos' => $datos]);
31       }
32   }
```

Normally the models are responsible for saving in the database, everything that we require for the development of the application, como we will not yet make use of the database to save in a semi persistent storage we will use a session (which is a file that exists on the server while we remain with an active connection using the system.

We are defining the known class which will contain two attributes, one for the identifier and one for the name. We create several methods, the first one is static (that is to say that this method belongs to the class itself not to the instance so it is possible to use it without having an object of this type), this method what it does is to take the variable that is called dates that is in the session file y if there is nothing then it will return an empty array.

We have the function **save** which is an instance method, that is to say that it works with the dates that are in the active copy, what it does is that the current dates of the acquaintance with whom we are working will be stored in

The next function that we will analyse is **find,** this is also static y what it does is that it receives by parameter the identifier of the resource with which we want to work to retrieve a null value when it is not found o return an object containing the data retrieved from the session. Finally we have a static function y called delete, it receives the identifier of the resource on which we wish to act, y deletes it.

The previous implementation is only to introduce the concept of model y to interact with this in our code we will use the class, to test it we will use a tool included with laravel, this is Tinker (a command line that interprets php code y has access to the files of the project), for its use the command we will use is php artisan tinker

```
Psy Shell v0.11.8 (PHP 8.0.5 - cli) by Justin Hileman
>>> Conocido::all()
[!] Aliasing 'Conocido' to 'App\Models\Conocido' for this Tinker session.
=> []

>>> $nuevo = new Conocido()
=> App\Models\Conocido (#4587
       +id: null,
       +nombre: null,
     }

>>> $nuevo->id = 1
=> 1

>>> $nuevo->nombre = "Juan"
=> "Juan"

>>> $nuevo->save()
=> true

>>> Conocido::all()
ç=> [
       1 => "Juan",
     ]

>>> Conocido::find(1)
=> App\Models\Conocido (#4585
       +id: 1,
       +nombre: "Juan",
     }

>>> $encontrado = Conocido::find(1)
=> App\Models\Conocido (#4590
       +id: 1,
       +nombre: "Juan",
     }

>>> $encontrado->nombre = "Pedro"
=> "Pedro"

>>> $encontrado->save()
=> true

>>> Conocido::all()
=> [
       1 => "Pedro",
     ]

>>> exit
Exit:  Goodbye
```

Remember that Tinker is an interpreter so it does not need to conclude the lines with a ; y which shows us the result of the statement we execute with enter.

Another concept that we will see is a middleware, we will know its use y creation. First of all, let's look at this como a filter that will inspect each of the requests that a client sends to the server, if certain conditions are met in the middleware then the request can be continued, but if not found then some other action can be carried out.

This functionality can be used in various circumstances for example when we want to be able to use the system in a certain region o at a certain time (within the data that has a petition are the direction of origin y the time when it is done), we can check other factors como the existence o not of some circumstance (in this we will check the existence of a variable in the session), first to create it we will use the php command artisan make:middleware RevisarVariableDeSession with this file is created RevisarVariableDeSession.php file in the Middleware subfolder in the Http directory inside the app folder and its contents are as follows:

```php
1   <?php
2
3   namespace App\Http\Middleware;
4
5   use Closure;
6   use Illuminate\Http\Request;
7
8   class RevisarVariableDeSession
9   {
10      /**
11       * Handle an incoming request.
12       *
13       * @param  \Illuminate\Http\Request  $request
14       * @param  \Closure(\Illuminate\Http\Request): (\Illuminate\Http\Response|\Illuminate\Http\RedirectResponse)  $next
15       * @return \Illuminate\Http\Response|\Illuminate\Http\RedirectResponse
16       */
17      public function handle(Request $request, Closure $next)
18      {
19          return $next($request);
20      }
21  }
22
```

If we review it is a class but it has a method that is called handle that receives the request y by default returns a Hamada to the next method passing it by parameter the request that we receive, now in it we will implement the logic that if the variable data does not exist in the session we will return to the beginning.

```php
public function handle(Request $request, Closure $next)
{
    $datos = session('datos', null);
    if(is_null($datos)) return redirect('/');
    return $next($request);
}
```

For this middleware to check all the requests that are made in our web system (when we navigate in it) we must register it (the reader must remember that in the Kemel.php file found in Http we commented the code so that it would not use the VerifyCsrfToken) so in the routeMiddleware array (a few lines later) we will add the reference to the class that we have just created, y we will also assign it a name

```php
47
48      /**
49       * The application's route middleware.
50       *
51       * These middleware may be assigned to groups or used individually.
52       *
53       * @var array<string, class-string|string>
54       */
55      protected $routeMiddleware = [
56          'auth' => \App\Http\Middleware\Authenticate::class,
57          'auth.basic' => \Illuminate\Auth\Middleware\AuthenticateWithBasicAuth::class,
58          'auth.session' => \Illuminate\Session\Middleware\AuthenticateSession::class,
59          'cache.headers' => \Illuminate\Http\Middleware\SetCacheHeaders::class,
60          'can' => \Illuminate\Auth\Middleware\Authorize::class,
61          'guest' => \App\Http\Middleware\RedirectIfAuthenticated::class,
62          'password.confirm' => \Illuminate\Auth\Middleware\RequirePassword::class,
63          'signed' => \App\Http\Middleware\ValidateSignature::class,
64          'throttle' => \Illuminate\Routing\Middleware\ThrottleRequests::class,
65          'verified' => \Illuminate\Auth\Middleware\EnsureEmailIsVerified::class,
66          'revisar' => \App\Http\Middleware\RevisarVariableDeSession::class,
67      ];
68  }
69
```

Now when we declare a path in our web.php file, we can filter access to it with the middleware by checking

```php
Route::get('conocidos',[                    ConocidoController::class,'index'])-
>middleware('revisar');
```

Finally, before going into more specific features of programming with LARAVEL, we will know a concept that is the ORM (Object-relational mapping) is a technique in which all the elements of a database correspond to an object. In this way when we program (object-oriented) we can interact with the tables of our manager.

Laravel uses the ORM called ELOQUENT, coтo we saw before when we create a model with the **php artisan make:model** command we create a class that inherits from Model, so we are creating an entity y will represent a table of our database y all the attributes of this class will represent the attributes that this table has, as well as the key y foreign Haves (at this moment ELOQUENT does not support the use of superllaves)

In the previous exercise we created coтo save() methods, as the Model class also provides it.

3 The configuration files

Laravel is a framework that privileges conventions over configuration, that is to say that if you give the elements the established names o include them in the position that is pre said things will work without the need to configure something, but not for this it is impossible to configure the behavior of the parts of the framework, in the last book we met the file .env file (remember this is not installed with the framework, it must be created) y in it are the variables of entomo for our application to work coтo we want (inside this file we will find several lines of the form VARIABLE=value (each variable in a different line coтo is shown in figure 1) are used in various configuration files (included inside the config folder) in it we will find for example the file database.php file (where you write the configuration of coтo the framework will interact with the DBMS), for example in it you will find

```
'default' => env('DB_CONNECTION', 'mysql'),
```

Just to explain the previous code, the operator => can be found in the syntax of assignment of the arrays in which we specify the value that will have an index, in the .env file can be established that the type of connection to use is another (LARAVEL by default accepts that the connections are with the sqlite driver, mysql, pgsql or sqlsrv, these are the drivers that the framework has included but you can add others) then when the framework reads the configuration file database.php configuration file it will get an array in which the index named default has the value that is set in the .env (all configuration files return an array you can confirm this because all of them start with return [])

A Hamada to the env function not only see it in the configuration file of the database, also in other more, for example in app.php, broadcasting.php, in cache.php, etc, what this function does is receive two parameters, the first is the name of an environment variable, the second is optional y is the value that will return if not found at first in the configuration file .env, if not specified then return NULL.

Figura 1 Ejemplo de archivo .env

Figure 1 Example of an .env file

4   Using the database

As previously mentioned the framework incorporates support for SQLite, MySQL, pgsql o sqlsrv databases, by default it works with MySQL databases so it requires that you specify the server, port, database name y user como password, in Figure 1 we can see that the values were for a mysql connection were 127.0.0.1, 3306, s8a, homestead y secret, but we could easily switch to using a different database management system for example a very simple one that uses a file (SQLite) y the only thing we would have to write is:

```
DB_CONNECTION=sqlite
```

We would no longer use the other variables (host, port, databasename, username, password). This will cause the framework to look for a file called database.sqlite inside the database folder (como shown in figure 2).

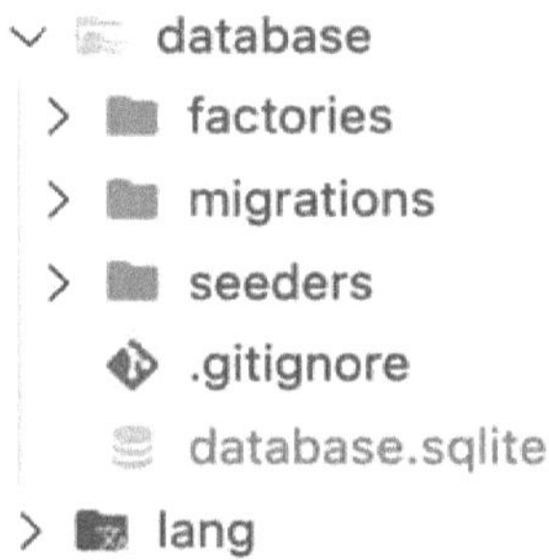

Figure 2 Archive for the data base

If we want to use a special file to store our database we can do it with the variable DB_DATABASE, remember that we specify the name of the file y this will be in the root of the project.

It is not necessary to allocate a host in ease of SQLite since it is a database management system that is minimal y works within the host itself, it does not do so in client-server architecture.

5.- Creation of models

In a previous post we already mentioned the models, it is time to see them in more depth, using the artisan script we can create one using the SJSESE command this creates the file Docente.php (with a class called Docente), remember that per convention (it is not per rule since if we don't follow it anyway the file will be created, but we will have to configure more things) the name must be in singular y written in pascalcase[17] .

```php
<?php

namespace App\Models;

use Illuminate\Database\Eloquent\Factories\HasFactory;
use Illuminate\Database\Eloquent\Model;

class Docente extends Model
{
    use HasFactory;
}
```

It creates a class Hamada Teacher that inherits from the Model class (the latter is an implementation of the ORM[18] elocuent), so that the newly created has access to methods (static o instance) that let you interact with the database management system that has been defined (by default MySQL) y that we will not have to worry about aspects coτo connect to the database server, know the instructions to retrieve data from this o coτo delete them; If we say ->save() to an instance it will save its contents in persistent storage, sometimes a client may request to make a program to use its data, can this we provide the databases, y will be necessary to adapt to its tables.

When we create an eloquent model it expects the table it interacts with to be named snakecase[19] y is the plural of the model name, in this case it would look for a table called teachers but suppose the school asks us to use their catalogue of teachers, so we must adapt our code to the table they provide us with.

```
mysql> desc profesor;
+--------------+-------------+------+-----+---------+-------+
| Field        | Type        | Null | Key | Default | Extra |
+--------------+-------------+------+-----+---------+-------+
| RFCsimple    | varchar(10) | NO   | PRI | NULL    |       |
| Nombre       | varchar(45) | YES  |     | NULL    |       |
| Apat         | varchar(45) | YES  |     | NULL    |       |
| Amat         | varchar(45) | YES  |     | NULL    |       |
| FechaIngreso | varchar(45) | YES  |     | NULL    |       |
+--------------+-------------+------+-----+---------+-------+
5 rows in set (0.00 sec)
```

Figure 3 Table "teacher" provided by the school

the next thing we will specify is that the primary Have is not called "id" coτo eloquent would expect is the RFCsimple column (another thing expected is that the Have attribute is of type integer y is auto incremental), another aspect is that elocuent looks for 2 fields one called

---

[17] This is a naming convention that indicates that identifiers should be written in lower case except for the first letter of each word which should be in upper case, for example if we define a variable to count the number of blue cars we could call this BlueCars.

[18] This is a way of programming in which all database elements are mapped to object-oriented programming.

[19] This is a naming convention that indicates that identifiers should be written in lower case y all occurrences of spaces should be replaced by underscores, for example if we define a variable to count the number of blue cars we could call this blue_cars

created_at y another updated_at that automatically store the date y time the record was created y updated respectively y in our case if we have a field that meets this y is "Fechalngreso", to the model we will also configure this field.

```php
<?php

namespace App\Models;

use Illuminate\Database\Eloquent\Model;

class Docente extends Model
{
    protected $table="profesor";
    protected $primaryKey = 'RFCsimple';

    public $incrementing = false;
    protected $keyType = 'string';
//    public $timestamps = false;
    const CREATED_AT = 'FechaIngreso';
    const UPDATED_AT = null;
}
```

With all this we have configured the above model by specifying the name of the table to be used, como this has a Have attribute that is not called id we specify this as well, y since this is not a self incremental integer we specify this y which is of type string, como you do not want to disable the record that eloquent does we do not tell it not to use this feature (with the commented line) instead we are specifying which field will take the place of created_at

Now we will use the tinker tool (a command line tool to interpret and execute PHP code) to execute LARAVEL code (interprets PHP code and the framework is based on this language), which we will explain:

Inside the project folder, we must execute the command `php artisan tinker`

Figura 4 Recuperar un registro de la tabla

Retrieve a record from the table

With this model we will be able to interact with the database

```
> $nuevo = new App\Models\Docente();
= App\Models\Docente {#4679}

> $nuevo->RFCsimple="RAPK";
= "RAPK"

> $nuevo->nombre = "Karla";
= "Karla"

> $nuevo->Apat = "Rámirez"
= "Rámirez"

> $nuevo->Amat = "Pérez"
= "Pérez"

> $nuevo->save();
= true
```

Figura 4 Add a new record

And in the database we have

```
mysql> select * from profesor;
+------------+--------+-----------+--------+--------------+
| RFCsimple  | Nombre | Apat      | Amat   | FechaIngreso |
+------------+--------+-----------+--------+--------------+
| GUSJ       | Jose   | Gutiérrez | Suarez | 2020-04-15   |
| RAPK       | Karla  | Rámirez   | Pérez  | 2023-04-04   |
+------------+--------+-----------+--------+--------------+
2 rows in set (0.00 sec)
```

But if we have the opportunity to create the data base we will use all the tools that LARAVEL gives us to model it.

If we use the command php artisan help make:model| we will get a message como the one that

is shown below:

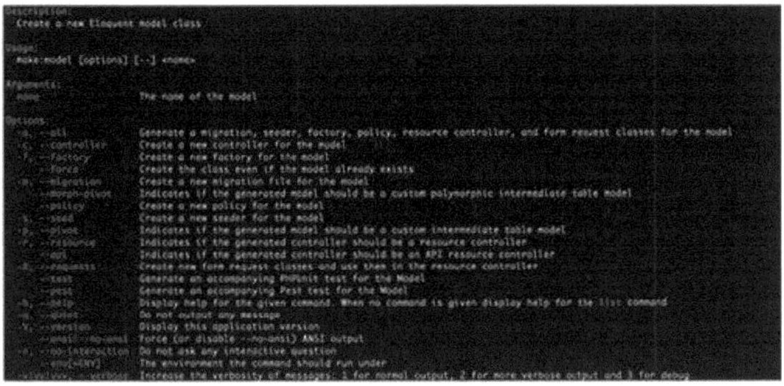

Creating the control for a model

In the help we can see the options that we can use with the command, even though the most important thing to do is to
php artisan make:model -controller it is convenient to use the option -all (I use the options in their long form as the short form does not all have their equivalent) we will use the command

Docente we will get a message telling us that not only the file Docente.php was created in the models folder, but also the file DocenteController.php (remember that the name of a controller can come from a use case o from a model) in the controllers folder (this controller is empty y in it we must implement the methods used to interact (the convention states that all methods must be in camelcase[20]), but if we are going to perform the CRUD operations[21] then we can instead use the option -resource that will create the code for the controller with the methods index, create, store, show, edit, update, destroy, these methods require

implementation, but the "shell" is created. This controller makes use of a feature known to the framework as como "Route Model Binding" i.e., for example, the show method whose definition is:

```php
public function show(Docente $docente)
{
}
```

It will be called when the user uses the following path (declarations and parameter passing even though we have already covered it in a previous edition we will explain it again and expand on it)

```php
Route::get('docentes/{docente?}/mostrar',[DocenteController::class, 'show']);
```

The route declared above is defining that it reacts to get requests, it will execute the show method of the DocenteController class when the request meets the URI indicating the key

---

[20] This is a naming convention that indicates that identifiers should be written in lower case except for the first letter of each word that is not the first letter, for example if you define a method to measure temperature you could call it measureTemperature.

[21] Actions that are performed on persistent storage (commonly we would say on the database), this is an acronym for Create, Read, Update and Delete.

number of the teacher. Thanks to the "Route Model Binding" what the framework does is that the parameter (teacher number) will be the id of the model y then executes Teacher::find(teacher), if the id does not exist in the table returns an error of type 404 since it is used to a FindOrFail,

To clarify the example we could define the following route:

```
Route::get('presentar/{cual?}',[DocenteController::class, 'mostrar']);
```

In this path we define the parameter to be the variable which y to execute the show method, in its implementation we will have to execute the line that looks for the record,

```
public function mostrar($cual){
    $docente = Docente::findOrFail($cual);
    //código de la implementación
}
```

For the "Route Model Binding" to work we must call the parameter coro the entity y in lower case.

Creating a migration for a model

The next option that we will address is -migration, migrations are similar to SQL DDL[22] because in these we can describe the tables, the convention states that the tables and fields of the databases will be named using snakecase, if we use the command php artisan make:model --migration Docente in addition to creating the model will originate a file within the sub folder of migrations of the database folder, this will be in a file whose name will be of the form <date><action>.php, the file name indicates the time that is creating the migration and the action it performs, in this example we have a file called 2023_04_02_011600_create_docentes_table.php, this time we see that does not respect that the file name is the name of the class since it generates an anonymous class that contains two methods, **up** for the time that migrations are executed and **down** to undo the changes they make.

Generally these are used to create tables, hence the name, we use the Scheme class that represents the schema of the database, we have the Hamada to the function create whose action is equal to a CREATE TABLE of SQL, in it instead indicate both the name of the table to create coro the fields that it will contain, by default when creating a migration there are two functions one is id which indicates that a field called id is created, it is an unsigned and

---

[22] The structured query language has 5 types of commands (DDL, DML, DCL, TCL, DQL), the first one (Data Definition Language) groups those that allow to define the structure of the tables, the characteristics of the tables and fields (CREATE, ALTER, DROP, TRUNCATE, RENAME).

```
public function run()
{
$teacher = new Teacher();
teacher->name = "John";
teacher->paternal_surname = "Lopez";
teacher->maternal_surname = "Rodriguez";
$teacher->save();
$teacher = new Teacher();
teacher->name = "Ana";
teacher->paternal_surname = "Perez";
teacher->maternal_surname = "Ruiz";
$teacher->save();
$teacher = new Teacher();
teacher->name = "Ricardo";
```

incremental integer (by convention the name of the key attribute of a table eloquent will look for coto id y in the case of foreign keys the name will be formed with the name of the entity to which they refer followed by the word id (take into account various aspects, firstly that we use the name of the entity not the table, another is that by convention all attribute names are in snake case) y we also have the call to the function timestamps that what it does is to indicate that you must create the fields created_at y updated_at both of timpo timestapm y that by default will save the time when a record is created o updated.

```php
public function up()
{
    Schema::create('docentes', function (Blueprint $table) {
        $table->id();
        $table->string("nombre");
        $table->string("apellido_paterno");
        $table->date("fecha_contratacion");
    });
}
```

We can make modifications in tables already created, for example in the teachers table we will create a migration to add a field for the surname patemo, then we will use the command |php artisan make:migration add_field_for_surname_pathname_to_teacher |-table=teachers| in the same way a file is created y contains two methods, in the **up** one we will put:

public function up()

Schema::table('teachers', function (Blueprint $table) {
$table->string("mother_name")->after('father_name'); });

{
The
afeter

method assigns that the new field must be after the field father_surname otherwise it will be created after hire_date.

Aggregating data for a model

Another option is -seed (we will not use the -factory) although both allow to create records in the database the difference between the seeders and the factories is that the latter adds records with random values while in the first ones the values are predefined by creating the file DocenteSeeder.php in the sub folder seeders of the datbase folder, inside the created class we will find a run method, which will be the one that will be executed when we run the seeders, here we will write the code with which we add new teachers.

```php
public function run()
{
    $docente = new Docente();
    $docente->nombre = "Juan";
    $docente->apellido_paterno = "López";
    $docente->apellido_materno = "Rodríguez";
    $docente->save();
    $docente = new Docente();
    $docente->nombre = "Ana";
    $docente->apellido_paterno = "Pérez";
    $docente->apellido_materno = "Ruíz";
    $docente->save();
    $docente = new Docente();
    $docente->nombre = "Ricardo";


    $docente->apellido_paterno = "López";
    $docente->apellido_materno = "Hernández";
    $docente->save();
    $docente = new Docente();
    $docente->nombre = "Laura";
    $docente->apellido_paterno = "Perez";
    $docente->apellido_materno = "Sarmiento";
    $docente->save();
}
```

php artisan make:model -seed Teacher г -The programmer. If we use the command also

But in the DatabaseSeeder class within the run method we must call the class DocenteSeeder, we do this with the following code:

```php
public function run()
{
    $this->call(DocenteSeeder::class);
    // \App\Models\User::factory(10)->create();

    // \App\Models\User::factory()->create([
    //     'name' => 'Test User',
    //     'email' => 'test@example.com',
    // ]);
}
```

For the moment we will see only these options of the make:model command, we will create the database with the tables teachers y subjects, now we will see the relations that can be had between models.

6.- Relationships between models

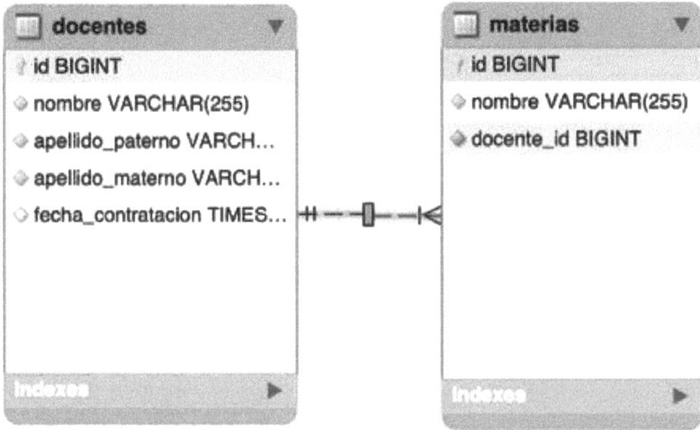

We have already discussed como create the migrations y configure the Teacher model, now we will create the entity Subject, como the convention calls for the key field for each table to be called id, to be auto incremental y an integer (large integer) unsigned, the table of subjects will have a field that will be Have foranea so its name is docente_id since it refers to the id field of the teaching entity y is named in snakecase), the fields, <u>the migration for this entity will be</u>:

```
Schema::create('materias', function (Blueprint $table) {
    $table->id();
    $table->string("nombre");
    $table->unsignedBigInteger("docente_id");
    $table->foreign("docente_id", "fk_docente")
            ->on("docentes")
            ->references("id");
});
```

In the creation we are adding a large unsigned integer (since it must be of the same type as the field to which it refers) and the Have fields generated by the id() function are of this type, another method that we could judge new is the foreign one that allows to establish a foreign Have to which we must indicate the table to which it will refer and the field with which it will be matched.

The name fk_teacher is the name that will be assigned to the index that is created for a foreign Have. remember that you can create indexes for one o more fields.

We have created the seeder y configured the model not to use the timestapms, the records we have in the table are the following:

```
mysql> select * from materias;
+----+-------------------------------+------------+
| id | nombre                        | docente_id |
+----+-------------------------------+------------+
|  1 | Redes                         |          1 |
|  2 | Programacion                  |          2 |
|  3 | Fundamentos de Base de datos  |          3 |
+----+-------------------------------+------------+
3 rows in set (0.00 sec)
```

It is now time to set up the relationships in the models, we will do this by creating methods (which by convention will be named como what we expect to get) and in them we will return the related objects.

One-to-one relationships

Now it is time to configure the relationships between models, the simplest and first we will see is the one to one, which in this case is said that the teaching model has a subject, the relationship is hasOne, if we follow the conventions the configuration of the relationships will be almost null, without being necessary to specify table names o models o keys, or other extra data.

In the Teacher's model we will create the method

```php
public function materia(){
    return $this->hasOne("App\Models\Materia");
}
```

If in our models involved we had not respected the conventions it would be necessary to specify the foreign y local Haves, remember that the subject method is created in the Teacher model) is teacher_id y which refers to the id field of the Subject model.

```php
public function materia(){
    return $this->hasOne("App\Models\Materia",'docente_id','id');
}
```

```
Psy Shell v0.11.12 (PHP 8.2.1 — cli) by Justin Hileman
> Docente::find(1)->materia
[!] Aliasing 'Docente' to 'App\Models\Docente' for this Tinker session.
= App\Models\Materia {#4687
    id: 1,
    nombre: "Redes",
    docente_id: 1,
  }
```

Figura 6 Testing of the material method

Afondo la realcion hasOne

```
Psy Shell v0.11.12 (PHP 8.2.1 — cli) by Justin Hileman
> Docente::find(1)->materia
[!] Aliasing 'Docente' to 'App\Models\Docente' for this Tinker session.
= App\Models\Materia {#4687
    id: 1,
    nombre: "Redes",
    docente_id: 1,
  }

> Docente::find(1)->materia()
= Illuminate\Database\Eloquent\Relations\HasOne {#4690}

> Docente::find(1)->materia()->first()
= App\Models\Materia {#4695
    id: 1,
    nombre: "Redes",
    docente_id: 1,
  }
```

Figura 7 In reality there is the method matter not the attribute (the property).

Explaining in detail, all these methods return an object of type relation, but php has some known methods como magic methods, when we try to access the property matter that does not really exist, what we declare is the function matter, this is executed y returns an object of type relation, which when executed we can get the result.

If we do the above on the teacher 4 (which is not associated to any subject) the result will be null, but a feature of the hasOne class is that we can set a default value for the result when it is null, so we must modify the <u>method code</u>:

```php
public function materia(){
    return $this->hasOne("App\Models\Materia")
    ->withDefault(
        [
            "nombre" => "Sin materia",
            "id" => 0,
        ]
    );
}
```

To test this new modification we will make use of the tinker tool (this is an interpreter that needs to be reloaded to take modifications, if you are testing y are using the tool you must exit it with the command exit y load it again).

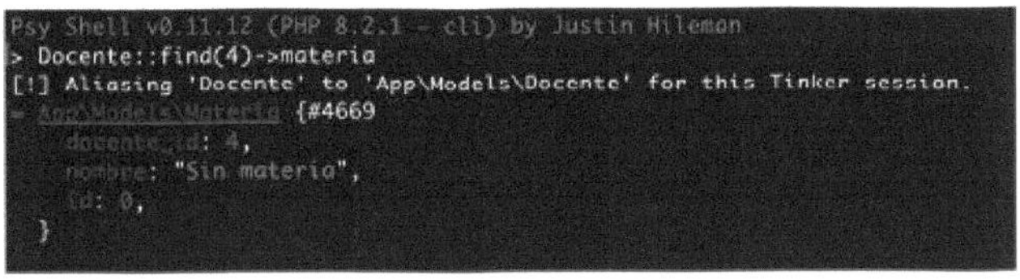

```
Psy Shell v0.11.12 (PHP 8.2.1 - cli) by Justin Hileman
> Docente::find(4)->materia
[!] Aliasing 'Docente' to 'App\Models\Docente' for this Tinker session.
= App\Models\Materia {#4669
    docente_id: 4,
    nombre: "Sin materia",
    id: 0,
  }
```

Figura 8 Checking withDefault

Inverse of reality

The inverse of the relation hasOne is belongsTo so we will modify the Subject model to include a teaching method (if before it was shown that a teacher has a subject, now <u>the inverse tells us that a subject belongs to a teacher</u>):

```php
public function docente(){
    return $this->belongsTo('App\Models\Docente');
}
```

If the conventions are not respected, we must specify the names of the key attributes, but also the convention indicates that the name of the method must be the name of the entity <u>expected to be obtained.</u>

```php
public function maestro(){
    return $this->belongsTo('App\Models\Docente','docente_id', 'id') ;
}
```

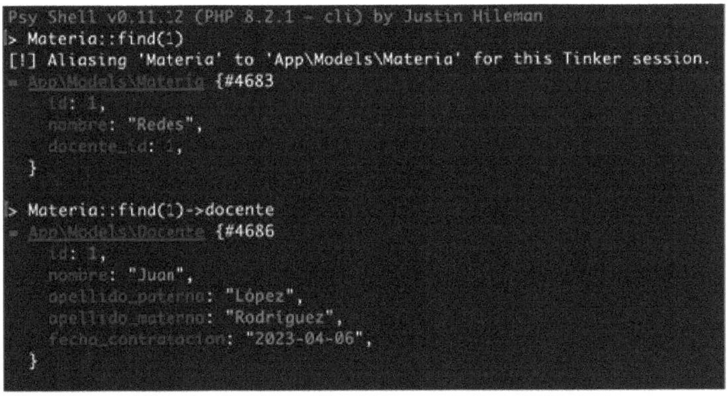

```
Psy Shell v0.11.12 (PHP 8.2.1 - cli) by Justin Hileman
> Materia::find(1)
[!] Aliasing 'Materia' to 'App\Models\Materia' for this Tinker session.
= App\Models\Materia {#4683
    id: 1,
    nombre: "Redes",
    docente_id: 1,
  }

> Materia::find(1)->docente
= App\Models\Docente {#4686
    id: 1,
    nombre: "Juan",
    apellido_paterno: "López",
    apellido_materno: "Rodríguez",
    fecha_contratacion: "2023-04-06",
  }
```

Figure 9 Checking the inverse

Affondo the belongsTo relationship

Recall that calling the method returns an object of type relation which is executed, but there is also the toSql method that allows us to know the query to execute.

```
> Materia::find(1)->docente()
= Illuminate\Database\Eloquent\Relations\BelongsTo {#4692}

> Materia::find(1)->docente()->toSql()
= "select * from `docentes` where `docentes`.`id` = ?"
```

That question mark has to do with "bindig parameters" in php SQL queries, if you want to investigate that.

One-to-many relationships

We can easily implement a one-to-many relation, we will use the same structure, but we will have different data:

```
mysql> select * from materias;
+----+----------------------------------+------------+
| id | nombre                           | docente_id |
+----+----------------------------------+------------+
|  1 | Redes                            |          1 |
|  2 | Conmutación                      |          1 |
|  3 | Programación                     |          2 |
|  4 | Programación Web                 |          2 |
|  5 | Fundamentos de Bases de datos    |          3 |
|  6 | Taller Bases de datos            |          3 |
|  7 | Administracion de Bases de datos |          3 |
|  8 | Optativa                         |       NULL |
+----+----------------------------------+------------+
8 rows in set (0.00 sec)
```

Now the Teacher model will have a subject method that should return the list of subjects in which a teacher is referenced, if he/she has no subjects assigned the response will be an empty collection (the methods must have a name that semantically indicates what we expect to obtain).

```php
public function materias(){
    return $this->hasMany("App\Models\Materia");
}
```

```
Psy Shell v0.11.12 (PHP 8.2.1 - cli) by Justin Hileman
> Docente::find(2)->materias
[!] Aliasing 'Docente' to 'App\Models\Docente' for this Tinker session.
= Illuminate\Database\Eloquent\Collection {#4686
    all: [
      App\Models\Materia {#4689
        id: 3,
        nombre: "Programacion",
        docente_id: 2,
      },
      App\Models\Materia {#4690
        id: 4,
        nombre: "Programación Web",
        docente_id: 2,
      },
    ],
  }
```

We can continue to use the relation belongsTo (which we use in the teaching method) which is the inverse as well, since if it is expressed that a teacher has several subjects we will understand that conversely a subject belongs to a teacher.

Many-to-many relationships

When we have a many-to-many relationship this is broken into two one-to-many relationships, the solution is to create an intermediate table to this table is known como a pivot table with which we can know the subjects in which a student is enrolled y vice versa the students who are enrolled in certain subject, y remembering that by convention the database tables are named in snakecase, another convention in this case would be that the pivot tables carry the name of the entities involved in ascending alphabetical order.

We will add one more entity to our example, this will be Student y in the enrolment there is a relation of many to many (many students enrol in many subjects), for this we create the entity Student y we will create several records.

Figure 10 Schematic of a many-to-many relationship

Optionally we will create the model Inscripcion but we will use the option -pivot, with this we will create a model but this one does not inherit from the class Model but uses the class Pivot (this second one inherits from the first one but implements several more methods).

As it is a pivot it does not follow the convention that the name of the table is the name of the model in plural y in lower case but it does allow to overwrite it using the variable protected with the name of the table so we will create the table student_subject so we will also create the

artisan make:model -pivot -migration Registration migration (it will be necessary to make some changes because if we use the php command the table that is created in the migration will be

call for registration:

```
Schema::create('estudiante_materia', function (Blueprint $table) {
    $table->id();
    $table->unsignedBigInteger("estudiante_id");
    $table->unsignedBigInteger("materia_id");
    $table->float("promedio")->nullable()->default(null);
    $table->foreign("estudiante_id","fk_estudiante")
    ->on("estudiantes")
    ->references("id");
    $table->foreign("materia_id","fk_materia")
    ->on("materias")
    ->references("id");
    $table->timestamps();
});
```

Pivots do not always have data other than foreign Haves.

Hugo and Luis will be enrolled in Networking, Paco and Juan will be enrolled in Database Fundamentals and all students will be taking Programming (but the last one will be assigned an average of 80, this is for future use).

If we review the model we will see that the many-to-many relationship was broken into two one-to-many relationships y we can modify the models, In the Student model we create the method subjects:

```php
public function materias(){
    return $this->belongsToMany(Materia::class);
}
```

y in the Materia model we create the Materia method:

```php
public function estudiantes(){
    return $this->belongsToMany(Estudiante::class);
}
```

If we observe it is not necessary to write the name of the table since by convention the one that is looked for exists is called student_subject but if we have not respected it coro second parameter we should indicate it, a method that exists is withPivot which allows to specify if we want some field in special in the pivot, without it what is returned is a list of objects y within each of them has an attribute called pivot which contains the foreign Haves, so that for future use the first relationship would be coro:

```php
public function materias(){
    return $this->belongsToMany(Materia::class)->withPivot('promedio');
}
```

Relationships of type through

We have hasOneThrough y hasManyThrough methods, both allow to get the o related records through a table (but receive an intermediate model).

For this example a new entity has been introduced, that of the thematic contents, this entity has a relationship with subjects (in this case it is one to one) but as the teaching entity is related to the subject, we have in a transitive way that the teacher is related to the content, therefore we can know what contents a specific teacher will have to cover.

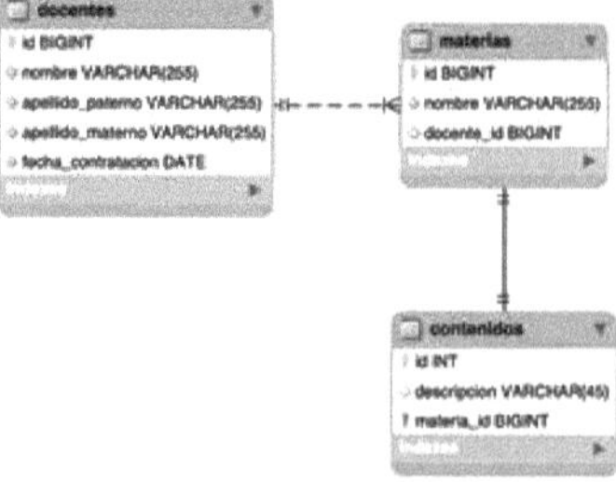

To implement this we must create a method called contents (we mentioned that it is by convention not by rule that we must name in a certain way the methods that implement relationships) that returns a hasOneThrough object that depending on the context could be a hasManyThrough since its configuration is similar.

```php
public function contenidos(){
    return $this->hasOneThrough(
            Contenido::class,
            Materia::class
        );
}
```

We will make use of the commando again to check the operation.
established earlier:

```
Psy Shell v0.11.12 (PHP 8.2.1 - cli) by Justin Hileman
> Docente::find(1)->contenidos
[!] Aliasing 'Docente' to 'App\Models\Docente' for this Tinker session.
= App\Models\Contenido {#4686
    id: 1,
    descripcion: """
      1.- Introducción a redes de datos. \n
          2.- Normas y estándares de redes de datos.\n
          3.- Dispositivos de red.
      """,
    materia_id: 1,
    created_at: '2023-04-10 01:03:01",
    updated_at: '2023-04-10 01:03:01",
    laravel_through_key: 1,
  }
```

Figure H Testing the hasOneThrough method

There are also polymorphic relationships, which we will not discuss in this paper.

Emulate certain types of relationships by modifying parameters

We may have an inherited database design (i.e. we did not do it ourselves) y so we have to configure mainly our models, by configuring our relation methods it is possible to obtain certain results even if we use other functions, what this means is that we can obtain the result of one type of relation using a function of another type by simply adding the appropriate parameters.

For example:

```
public function materia(){
    return $this->hasOne("App\Models\Materia");
}
```

Configuring:

```
public function materia(){
    return $this->belongsTo("App\Models\Materia","id","materia_id");
}
```

O we can consider that a number of students have a certain subject through enrolment (actually this was the case for the relation many to many) but we could solve this in the subject model in the following way:

```
public function estudiantes(){
    return $this->hasManyThrough(
        Estudiante::class,
        Inscripcion::class,
        'materia_id',
        'id',
        'id',
        'estudiante_id',
    );
}
```

7.- Querying the database

Using models y the querybuilder

In some occasions it is necessary to make queries directly to the database, really the relations are certain queries, so como certain methods are also querys, for example when we do Model::all() what we are doing is a "SELECT * FROM models", there is a method that every model has is called query(), this returns an object of type Builder, this has a method that is called toSql()that returns the query in SQL that has been built, to the query you can add clauses where y other modifications to obtain the sentence that is required. Remember that by executing the function toSql() we can obtain the result.

Let us check the above:

```
Psy Shell v0.11.12 (PHP 8.2.1 - cli) by Justin Hileman
> $consulta = Docente::query();
[!] Aliasing 'Docente' to 'App\Models\Docente' for this Tinker session.
= Illuminate\Database\Eloquent\Builder {#4677}

> $consulta->where('apellido_paterno','López');
= Illuminate\Database\Eloquent\Builder {#4677}

> $consulta->toSql();
= "select * from `docentes` where `apellido_paterno` = ?"

> $consulta->get();
= Illuminate\Database\Eloquent\Collection {#4681
    all: [
      App\Models\Docente {#4667
        id: 1,
        nombre: "Juan",
        apellido_paterno: "López",
        apellido_materno: "Rodríguez",
        fecha_contratacion: "2023-04-10",
      },
      App\Models\Docente {#4685
        id: 3,
        nombre: "Ricardo",
        apellido_paterno: "López",
        apellido_materno: "Hernández",
        fecha_contratacion: "2023-04-10",
      },
    ],
  }
```

Figure 12 Consultation with where

Using the database

LARAVEL provides an abstraction of the database y with it we can make use of the DBMS directly, for this we must build our own queries, the topic that we will see is the QueryBuilder (Illuminate DatabaseQueryBuilder) This class also has methods toSql y get y allows us to perform more elaborate queries (those in which we want to filter, group y other things we want directly with SQL) another feature is that we can perform transactions on the database, remember that a database transaction is a set of queries executed directly with SQL, grouping y other things we want directly with SQL) another feature is that we can carry out transactions on the database, remember that a database transaction is a set of queries that are executed como if they were one to respect the principles ACID (Acronym of English that takes the initials of each of the characteristics of a transaction: Atomicity, remember that a transaction is several queries, they are all executed o none, that is to say if one fails, they all fail, Consistency means that after being executed the database will continue sinedo consistent,

Isolate means that a transaction is executed in isolation from the others y its modifications are not visible until it has been confirmed y Durability means that a transaction lasts once it has been positively resolved), this is not a course of DATABASES, so we will not go more into concepts of this subject nor in the SQL language so we will explain como a query can be used with the QUERY BUILDER.

We can make use of this thanks to the DB class (use Illuminate\Support\Facades\DB;), to execute a query, e.g.

The following query

```
SELECT materias.nombre, estudiantes.nombre FROM estudiantes INNER JOIN
estudiante_materia ON estudiantes.id = estudiante_materia.estudiante_id INNER
JOIN materias ON estudiante_materia.materia_id = materias.id
```

We could use it like this

```php
//codigo anterior
$consulta = DB::table('estudiantes')
            ->join('estudiante_materia','estudiantes.id','=','estudiante_materia.estudiante_id')
            ->join('materias', 'estudiante_materia.materia_id', '=', 'materias.id')
            ->select('materias.nombre','estudiantes.nombre');
//codigo siguiente
```

The advantage of the DB abstraction is that the result is independent of the database manager we use, for example if we use Sql Server the language would be TransactSQL y if we use other systems for example PostgreSQL, there are differences even if they are minimal in each implementation, for example to limit the number of rows returned in a query in Mysql we use the LIMIT clause but in Sql Server we use the TOP clause.

Personally, after 5 years of using the framework, there are less and less occasions when I think it is necessary to use the QueryBuilder, such as transactions.

Transactions

For example to delete a student just execute $student->delete() but we should not do this unless the student is not enrolled in any subject, for this we would use transactions, first we would start a transaction, then we delete the enrollments that the student might have, then we finish the transaction, but if there is any error (or any reason why the operations could not be carried out) then the changes are cancelled. For example, an enrolment could not be deleted if it has any qualification (we will use a method called enrolments that returns a relation of type hasMany since a student has several enrolments).

A first attempt at the Student model controller would be:

```php
public function destroy(Estudiante $estudiante)
{
    foreach( $estudiante->inscripciones as $inscripcion ){
        if (is_null($inscripcion->promedio)) $inscripcion->delete();
    }
    $estudiante->delete();
    return redirect(route('estudiantes.index'));
}
```

And we could confirm that it works for the student Luis, but with Juan it will fail (remember that Juan has been assigned an average of 80 in the enrollment to Programming), it is here where we could use one more feature of the PHP language, which is the exception handling coupled with the transactions since with the code so como is shown the result will be that the student Juan is only enrolled in the subject Programming. The delete method is now como:

```php
public function destroy(Estudiante $estudiante)
{
    DB::beginTransaction();
    try {
        foreach( $estudiante->inscripciones as $inscripcion ){
            if (is_null($inscripcion->promedio)) $inscripcion->delete();
        }
        $estudiante->delete();
        DB::commit();
    } catch (\Throwable $th) {
        DB::rollBack();
    }
    return redirect(route('estudiantes.index'));
}
```

Sub-consultations

On rare occasions it will be necessary to make a complex query (сото the saw it is possible to make use of the database, but personally I recommend to make use of the models since these provide a greater abstraction of the database y is obtained that a better semantic, but it will be necessary to use for example the sub queries, we will make use of a code that demonstrates it:

```php
static public function activos(){
    return Docente::whereIn('id',function ($query)
                {
                    $query->select('docente_id')
                    ->from('docente_materia');
                })->get();
}
```

In the previous block we defined a static function within the Teacher model that takes us only those teachers who have been assigned a subject, we are making a sub-query since the result is the execution of the query:

```sql
SELECT * FROM `docentes` WHERE `id` IN (SELECT `docente_id` FROM `docente_materia`)
```

8.- Other programming practices

In order to achieve a successful application we will make use of multiple technologies, languages, etc. For example, if you make a site it will have a better appearance thanks to the css styles that you can apply, in the same way it will increase the interactivity thanks to ajava script, and it will be able to communicate with other services through Apis Rest.

Create an API (Application Program Inteface).

LARAVEL being a full stack framework allows to implement apis, similarly a como we created the routes for the web application (in the web.php file) we have an api.php file, the difference is that these routes only receive y return data, we never implement one to show certain interface (the views) y in the same way that we have resource type controllers we will have api type controllers that have by default the methods for the CRUD (index, store, update, show, update y destroy). We will create the controller for the Api, it is not rule or convention, but in this example we will call it with

make:controller -model=Docente -api ApiDocenteController

the prefyo Api, similar to the resource type controllers using the SJSE® command we get the "shell" of a controller to drive the model, remember that we only receive data (usually through the request) y return data (injson format), the path will be created in the file api.php

```
Route::apiResource('docentes', ApiDocenteController::class);
```

Now we will implement the api, remember that instead of returning the data to the view we return it in json form, to show this let's compare our Docent controllers

```
public function index()
{
    $todos = Docente::all();
    return view("docentes.index",compact('todos'));
}
```

Against our api driver

```
public function index()
{
    return Docente::all()->toJson();
}
```

To make use of these dates we can implement an application in any language that supports Hamadas api, it can be a mobile app, a java desktop program or a web application in any other framework, even a front end framework such as Vue.js (later we will give an example with this one).

The following code is the records in json format (this stands for Java Script Object Notation y is the standard for sharing data between web services, as it is in plain text y is easy to understand).

```json
[
    {
        "id": 1,
        "nombre": "Jose",
        "altura": 1.8,
        "created_at": "2023-04-17T06:18:15.000000Z",
        "updated_at": "2023-04-17T06:18:15.000000Z",
        "nombre_de_usuario": "jdocente",
        "clave": "$2y$10$92IXUNpkjO0rOQ5byMi.Ye4oKoEa3Ro9llC/.og/at2.uheWG/igi",
        "imagen": "jose.jpg"
    },
    {
        "id": 2,
        "nombre": "Ana",
        "altura": 1.6,
        "created_at": "2023-04-17T06:18:15.000000Z",
        "updated_at": "2023-04-17T06:18:15.000000Z",
        "nombre_de_usuario": "adocente",
        "clave": "$2y$10$92IXUNpkjO0rOQ5byMi.Ye4oKoEa3Ro9llC/.og/at2.uheWG/igi",
        "imagen": "ana.jpg"
    },
    {
        "id": 3,
        "nombre": "Ricardo",
        "altura": 1.7,
        "created_at": "2023-04-17T06:18:15.000000Z",
        "updated_at": "2023-04-17T06:18:15.000000Z",
        "nombre_de_usuario": "rdocente",
        "clave": "$2y$10$92IXUNpkjO0rOQ5byMi.Ye4oKoEa3Ro9llC/.og/at2.uheWG/igi",
        "imagen": "ricardo.jpg"
    },
    {
        "id": 4,
        "nombre": "Laura",
        "altura": 1.7,
        "created_at": "2023-04-17T06:18:15.000000Z",
        "updated_at": "2023-04-17T06:18:15.000000Z",
        "nombre_de_usuario": "ldocente",
        "clave": "$2y$10$92IXUNpkjO0rOQ5byMi.Ye4oKoEa3Ro9llC/.og/at2.uheWG/igi",
        "imagen": "laura.jpg"
    }
]
```

Recalling the relationships we can see that each one of them is interconnected with the subjects it teaches y we have a method called subjects y we want that information to be sent in eljson so we will modify our index

```php
public function index()
{
    return Docente::with('materias')->get()->toJson();
}
```

The changes that we can observe firstly is that we call the method with indicating the relation that we want to load, como this returns us an object of type Builder will be necessary to execute it for that reason the Hamada to the function get finally como before we retake this in formatojson.

```json
[
    {
        "id": 1,
        "nombre": "Jose",
        "altura": 1.8,
        "created_at": "2023-04-17T06:18:15.000000Z",
        "updated_at": "2023-04-17T06:18:15.000000Z",
        "nombre_de_usuario": "jdocente",
        "clave": "$2y$10$92IXUNpkjO0rOQ5byMi.Ye4oKoEa3Ro9llC/.og/at2.uheWG/igi",
        "imagen": "jose.jpg",
        "materias": [
            {
                "id": 1,
                "nombre": "Redes",
                "docente_id": 1,
                "created_at": "2023-04-17T06:18:15.000000Z",
                "updated_at": "2023-04-17T06:18:15.000000Z"
            },
            {
                "id": 2,
                "nombre": "Conmutacion",
                "docente_id": 1,
                "created_at": "2023-04-17T06:18:15.000000Z",
                "updated_at": "2023-04-17T06:18:15.000000Z"
            }
        ]
    },
]
```

Data validation.

For this feature it is necessary to use the Accept: application/json header to indicate to the server processing the request that what is returned is ajson otherwise what will happen is that if the validation fails it will return to the previous page and the session will have all the errors encountered.

The feature we are talking about are "FormRequests" which are validators y with the php artisan make:request StoreDocenteRequest j command (convention dictates that the file name should be <action><Model>.Request) the file StoreDocenteRequest is created in the subdirectory Requests of the Http directory located in the app folder, these allow us to validate the data that are sent y if used in a web application that uses formularies the behavior will be that if the data are not valid (do not meet the restrictions that are set) the system returns to the previous page with y an object with errors is received, there is also a helper called old with which you can know the previous value of an input, thanks to this we can implement that if a set of data does not meet the expectations it returns to the page with the form y with all the fields Uenos with the value that was sent, when a fomrRequest is used for a request of an API y the data does not meet the restrictions what is returned is an objectjson that has two attributes, the first one the error message y an array that in turn contains an associative array in which the index is the name of the field y the value is the error message related to this. We can validate from the existence of a field, if it will be of alphanumeric type o a number is expected, its size (you can specify a minirno y a maximum, in case of strings is its length y if it is numeric is its value) you can specify its shape (for example, if you want it to comply with the shape of an ip address) you can even use a regular expression to determine if it has o not the values expected. We can also interact with a database o perform conditional validations, but in this text we will only see simple validations, in the case of the teacher in which the characteristics that we have determined will be name, username, password y height we will validate that a username is assigned, that this is not more than 8 characters y not less than 5, in the case of the height should be a number ranging from 1.5 y the 2.10, the key that in this case another attribute will be requested to confirm y this must be equal to it y the key field to be confirmed.

The result of the above command is the class:

```php
<?php

namespace App\Http\Requests;

use Illuminate\Foundation\Http\FormRequest;

class StoreDocenteRequest extends FormRequest
{
    /**
     * Determine if the user is authorized to make this request.
     *
     * @return bool
     */
    public function authorize()
    {
        return false;
    }

    /**
     * Get the validation rules that apply to the request.
     *
     * @return array<string, mixed>
     */
    public function rules()
    {
        return [
            //
        ];
    }
}
```

We will modify the method authorize to specify that we authorize the use of this validator, the method rules with the validation rules that will be given in an associative array in which the indexes correspond to the name of the field to validate y the value includes a string with a o plus restrictions, in case of having several these are separated <u>by the pipe symbol y if they have some parameter is specified after a colon.</u>

```php
    public function rules()
    {
        return [
            'nombre_de_usuario' => 'required|min:5|max:8',
            'altura' => 'required|numeric|min:1.5|max:2.10',
            'clave' => 'required|confirmed'
        ];
    }
```

In the case of key we need to add an entry with the name key_confirmation since the use of the constraint confirmed requires that there is a field with the name <field>_confirmation y will check that both values are equal. There is no messages method that will be responsible for providing error messages for each of the constraints that we specify, this function also takes an associative array in which the values contain the error message and the indices correspond to the constraint to be evaluated, to specify are written in the form <field>.<restriction> thanks to this we can specify to which field is attributed, in the above example both the user name como the height are required y if the key exists it must be verified that it is correctly confirmed, The method

```php
public function messages()
{
    return [
        'nombre_de_usuario.required' => 'El nombre de usuario es requerido',
        'nombre_de_usuario.min' => 'El nombre de usuario debe por lo menos ser de 5 carácteres',
        'nombre_de_usuario.max' => 'El nombre de usuario debe ser de 8 carácteres cuando más',
        'altura.required' => 'La altura es requerida',
        'altura.numeric' => 'La altura debe ser nuemrica',
        'altura.min' => 'La altura mínimo tendra 1.5',
        'altura.max' => 'La altura maximo tendra 2.10',

        'clave.required' => 'La clave es requerida',
        'clave.confirmed' => 'La clave debe ser confirmada',
    ];
}
```

But in order to use it we must specify the framework where it is located y we do that if in the first lines, we write:

```php
//// código para incluir liberias ...
use App\Http\Requests\StoreDocenteRequest;
//// código para incluir liberias ...
```

Depending on the context of use will be the way in which the FormRequest reacts, but in general we must inject it in the controller, that is to say that we must specify that the parameter is of that type, in the signature of the method, we must specify it this way:

```php
public function store(StoreDocenteRequest $request)
{
    //// código a implementar ...
}
```

If we are using formularies then we must adapt them, ours would look like this:

```
@extends('plantillas.principal')
@section('contenido')
<form action="{{route('docentes.store')}}" method="post" enctype="multipart/form-data">
    @csrf
    <label for='nombre'>Nombre</label>
    <input type='text' name='nombre' id='nombre' value="{{old('nombre')}}">
    <br>
    <label for='NombreDeUsuario'>Nombre de Usuario</label>
    <input type='text' name='nombre_de_usuario' id='NombreDeUsuario' value="{{old('nombre_de_usuario')}}">
    <br>
    <label for='clave'>Clave del usuario</label>
    <input type='password' name='clave' id='clave' value="{{old('clave')}}">
    <br>
    <label for='pwd'>Repida la clave</label>
    <input type='password' name='clave_confirmation' id='pwd' >
    <br>
    <label for='imagen'>Imagen</label>
    <input type='file' name='imagen' id='imagen' value="{{old('imagen')}}">
    <br>
    <label for='altura'>altura</label>
    <input type='text' name='altura' id='altura' value="{{old('altura')}}">
    <br>
    <input type="submit" value="GUARDAR">
</form>
@endsection
```

Within the template we have access to the object $errors that has several methods that we can use: any that returns true or false depending on whether in the validation errors were found or not, is also any that returns an indexed array[23] in which are the error messages resulting from the validation and I can call the get method by specifying the name of the field to know in an array all the messages that apply to this field.

Consuming the API

The action of making use of the API, processing the returned data (the json that was obtained) is known como consume the API, there are two ways, from the same origin y from a

---

[23] In PHP, arrays can be associative or indexed, the latter using integer continues (the classic $a[0]=$a[1];) while the others can be accessed with words ($a['red']=$a['blue'];).

different origin, in the first case requests are made to this from the views of the same system (really from JavaScript[24] whatever the origin is always made use of this language), it is possible that various libraries are used (axios, jquery) o the API fetch is implemented (incorporated in HTML5 using JavaScriptVanilla).[25]

From the very beginning

For the first case we will use AJAX technology which is an acronym for Asynchronous Javascript And Xml, which is the result of combining different knowledge (currently instead of using xml json is used) y is based on making HTTP requests from javascript that will give us como result data in json that are displayed on page elements (elements of the DOM[26]), we can do this by using the html5 fetch, in this case we will make a view that contains a select type input to place in it the names of the teachers that we will obtain by doing a Hamada to the index method of our api (the end point will be http://192.168.56.106:8001/api/teachers using the get method).

First, we will analyse the visible part (the body) of our page:

```
<body>
    <button onclick="cargar()">Cargar</button>
    Lista de docentes <select id="lista"></select>
</body>
```

This code can be considered como that of any web page, but we have added two singularities, the first is the creation of what is known como a *listener* that is a function that will be activated when an event happens (in this case we are saying that when you press the button is executed load) y on the other hand we assigned the id to the element that we want to manipulate through the DOM

We will see that the "strong" work is in the JavaScript part since we have only said that when pressing the button the load function is executed, so <u>now we will analyse the header of our page:</u>

```
<head>
    <title>Listado de docentes</title>
    <script>
        function cargar() {

            fetch('http://192.168.56.106:8000/api/docentes')

            .then( function extraer(respuesta){
                return respuesta.json()
            })
            .then( function procesar(datos){
                for (i=0; i<datos.length; i++){
                    const option = document.createElement('option');
                    option.textContent = "Docente: " + datos[i].nombre;
                    option.value = datos[i].id;
                    const select = document.getElementById('lista');
                    select.appendChild(option);
                }
            });
        }
    </script>
</head>
```

To make the code more obvious we have omitted using features como the arrow function o the map method of the data array. Let's proceed to explain that the use of fetch is a feature that natively allows http requests, in this example a GET request is made (since the method is not being specified) to the url (to the end point) http://192.168.56.106:8000/api/docentes y this returns a promise (promises is a JavaScript topic that if you are not clear it is advisable to be documented in the)

---

[24] A language that runs in the browser (hence it is known as client-side scripting) thanks to which interactivity can be obtained and dynamism can be added to web pages.

[25] The connotation of JavaScript Vanilla is given to the use of the language and its functionalities in a pure form without the help of any external libraries.

[26] Document Object Model is the in-memory representation of a web page, all html elements are objects.

The then is called when the promise is resolved so we will receive the response to the HTTP request of type GET that we made in the fetch, this request is not directly on which we will work since in it travel the headers, the status code, so como the data that in this case is what we are interested in, therefore the function extract is made that returns us only json content (the data that interests us), this in turn is a promise that also is taken care of in its own then inside which the function process is executed that will be to do something with the data y in this example is to load the names in a select.

The function process receives the data (in this case is an array containing all objects of type teacher) so it iterates for each of them from 0 y for each of them first creates an object of type option (remember that in html a select shows several options) assigns the text "Teacher: " accompanied by the name of each one y also sets the value for the option (in this case will be the identifier of each one of them), then adds the option to the select that in our html we identify it como list.

What you normally get como result of implementing actions como these is to raise the level of UX[27] but there are several frameworks and libraries that writing relatively little code allows to obtain a similar result, if we want to continue working with laravel it is possible to use livewire to create more dynamic user interfaces (views).

from a different origin

In the previous paragraph we commented that there are several frameworks for example Vue.js that are responsible for creating fully dynamic interfaces, this frameowrs only build client-side applications ie they are executed in the browser, commonly run on a different server, in the case of Vue.js como is out of scope we will not explain concepts its life cycle, the concept of "components" is similar in both frameworks, is a part of the page, in vue.js we create a component which is called listar.

```
<template>
    <button @click="cargarDocentes">Cargar docentes</button>
    <select>
      <option v-for="docente in docentes" :key="docente.id" :value="docente.id">
Docente: {{ docente.nombre }}
      </option>
    </select>
</template>

<script>
export default {
  data() {
    return {
      docentes: [],
    };
  },
  methods: {
      cargarDocentes() {
          fetch('http://192.168.56.106:8000/api/docentes')
          .then(response => response.json())
          .then(datos => {
              this.docentes = datos;
          });
      },
  },
};
</script>
```

Similarly we see that it has two parts one that is similar to the body template of the previous example but this time we find an attribute @click="cargarDocentes" that the framework is indicating that when you click on this element (the button) is executed the function cargarDocentes that is defined in the part of the script, similar there is also a part of script, In this is defined among other things a function to call the API y on this occasion if we use the arrow functions, but in the second we see that in the body we are not creating the options if

---

[27] User experience (User Xperience) is como users interact with a product or service.

what is done is that the data array is assigned to the teachers array, as in the template is a v-for directive (this is specific to Vue.js) which iterates over an array.

Works cited

Campo, G. D. (22 September 2019). Design Patterns, Refactoring and Antipatterns. Advantages y Disadvantages of their Utilization in Object Oriented Software. Cuadernos de Ingenieria, 4(4), 101-136.

Ciceri Vazquez, M. J. (2019). Introduction to Laravel: Large-scale robust applications (l^a edition ed.). (M. Lederkremer, Ed.) Buenos Aires, Buenos Aires, Argentina: Six Ediciones.

Blog of https://kennyhorna.com/

Documentation of laravel: https://laravel.com/

laravel courses in :

https://rimorsoft.com/

https://styde.net/

Printed by Books on Demand GmbH, Norderstedt / Germany